MARCEL PROUST

MARCEL PROUST

From a photograph taken in Paris

MARCEL PROUST

by

CHARLOTTE HALDANE

London

ARTHUR BARKER LTD.

First published 1951

MADE AND PRINTED IN GREAT BRITAIN BY
MORRISON AND GIBB LIMITED, LONDON AND EDINBURGH

CONTENTS

To

W. SOMERSET MAUGHAM

DEAR WILLIE,

      In recollection of many delightful discussions in times past, of Marcel Proust and his masterpiece, I venture to dedicate this little study to you, in admiration and affection.

CHARLOTTE.

1.11.1950

CHAPTER I

BRIEF CANDLE

IN attempting to write of Marcel Proust, the man, the biographer or the critic has to contend with one insuperable rival and competitor : Marcel Proust, the author. For the enormously long novel which has placed him for all time among France's foremost writers has a dual personality, a twofold aspect. *A La Recherche du Temps Perdu* is at one and the same time a great novel and an even greater autobiography. No other author has used the events and experiences and memories of his own lifetime so fully, so exhaustively, as did Marcel Proust.

For this reason I shall not attempt here, at the beginning of this brief study, to give a detailed account of his outwardly uneventful life. The main content of that life was psychological, and it is impossible to analyse it adequately without constantly referring to his own version of his development, to his own self-portrait. For clarity's sake, therefore, I prefer, at this initial stage, to give the reader only a preliminary sketch, a short factual account of his background, his parentage and environment—an anatomical outline, as it were. The flesh-and-blood man, the physiological and psychological man will, I hope, reveal himself gradually, and emerge in due course, as he does at the end of *A La Recherche du Temps Perdu*, fully dressed, clothed in the strange garments of his own fantastic fashioning.

Marcel Proust was born on 10 July 1871. If ever there was a writer in the making of whom nature and nurture, heredity and environment, played the decisive part, it was he. There have been novelists and poets whose creative output seems to have little or no biological or social background. One thinks, for example, of that Polish sea captain, Joseph Conrad, who wrote some of the finest descriptive prose in the English language ; or of that most exotic of the great French lyric poets, Arthur Rimbaud, whose genius flowered, like some strange surrealist orchid, in the mud of Belgium. But if one might be inclined to deduce, from such examples, that literary talent has no regional or intellectual background, such an assumption would be nullified by the case of Marcel Proust. For he was intensely and intimately a son of France and a child of Paris. He was the product of his own period, as much as the great dramatist, Racine, or his own favourite memoirist, Saint-Simon. And his life and his life-work were stamped by the imprint of his own particular chronic ill-health and neurasthenia.

Marcel Proust is an almost perfect illustration of the fact that " the child is father to the man." For, like his characters, he never changed ; he simply grew, developing in adolescence and in manhood his latent physical and mental qualities. As in Oriental countries small boys are betrothed almost before they begin to learn their letters, so Marcel as a little boy became betrothed to chronic ill-health. There was something almost symbiotic in his relationship with his respiratory disorder ; it seems to have been fastened to him as the orchid or the fungus is fastened to its tree. Probably in all pathological conditions the sufferer's mind is influenced as profoundly as his body. But, whatever the general principles involved may be, in Proust's particular case there is no doubt at all about it ; his infirmity was as much mental as physical, and dominated his entire attitude to life. His frail body was, from the age of four, racked by acute asthma, he was subject to recurrent hay fever, and he endured, psychologically, the most extreme nervous tension and hypersensitivity.

On his father's side, Proust came of a family that for generations had been anchored to the little town of Illiers, near Chartres. Professor Adrien Proust was the first in the line to break with the family's narrow provincial tradition. He was a man of robust health, of considerable intelligence and professional distinction, who became a fashionable and prosperous medical consultant in Paris. In due course he gravitated from the practice of medicine to " hygiene "—a form of applied prophylaxis then almost in its infancy. Professor Proust was a medical scientist. He became head of the French medical health service ; held the first chair of Public Health in the French Faculty of Medicine, and it is to him that we owe the expression " cordon sanitaire."

The elder son of this man of great mental and physical vitality was the sickly neurasthenic Marcel. His younger son, Robert, however, was a thoroughly healthy boy who in due course grew up to distinction in his father's profession.

Their mother was a beautiful Jewess, Jeanne Weil, a girl of cultured and well-to-do family, with whom Dr. Adrien Proust had fallen in love when he was a rising young medical man in Paris. The Weil family came from Alsace. In the year 1870, when this noble French province was torn from the arms of France by the conquering Prussians—by the first great army of the Emperor William I, by Bismarck's daringly successful policy of German expansion, backed by von Moltke's military skill—Adrien Proust married Jeanne Weil. It was actually on their wedding day, 1 September 1870, that France suffered one of her most tragic and humiliating disasters, the capitulation of the French forces at Sedan. Then followed the ghastly siege of Paris, accompanied by starvation and disease, and the culminating terror of the Commune.

It would, I think, be rash to assume that Marcel inherited his hypersensitivity, his extraordinary receptivity to sensory and aesthetic stimuli, his orientally luxuriant imagination, and his physical weakness, directly, or exclusively, from his mother. The racial explanation of the inheritance of such characteristics is superficial and unscientific. It is possible that his nervous system was adversely influenced pre-natally by his mother's unusually harrowing experiences during pregnancy; but these were shared by all other Parisian mothers of the period, most of whom nevertheless produced physically robust and mentally uninteresting offspring.

Like most Parisians, Dr. Proust did not lose touch with his home, and during Marcel's childhood the family spent many long summers at Illiers, which later the author, Proust, was to immortalise—with its hawthorns and water-lilies, its church and its steeple, its little shut-in houses and its narrow-minded people—as " Combray."

Marcel Proust was born in the first year of the Third Republic. They both appeared on the European scene at a moment when the greatness of France seemed threatened with decline; after the capitulation at Sedan, and the battles of the Commune, the glories of the Paris of the second Empire seemed about to be engulfed in ignominious gloom. But the Europe and the France of those days had by no means exhausted the riches accumulated during the preceding years of industrial and capitalistic expansion. They were in fact still accumulating, at compound interest. In consequence, the young Republic was to lead in a period of economic stability, of cultural distinction, of luxurious living, of increasing liberalism in thought, power in science, and daring in art, that were characteristic of the last great era of bourgeois tranquillity, and were to endure until the outbreak of the first world war, in 1914.

In spite of the fact that Marx and Engels had published

the Communist Manifesto in 1848, and that their followers
had in the days of the Commune made their first terrific
assault on the bastions of bourgeois Paris ; in spite of the
subsequent emergence of a strong social-democratic political
trend, class distinction and rigid social convention remained
and were to remain dominant in Parisian social circles for
almost the whole of Proust's lifetime. The forty-three
years from 1871 until 1914 were to provide the setting for
the major part of Marcel Proust's life and creation. He
grew into adolescence and maturity stamped with the
imprint of this period and of the rich cultural develop-
ments, the social habits and customs, that were unfolding
within it.

French society, in his time, was rigidly divided into groups
and castes that had few meeting-places in common. The
ancient nobility, the remaining descendants of the great
princely and feudal houses, withdrew with upswept skirts
into the Faubourg Saint-Germain, where they still attempted
to preserve themselves from social contamination by the
upstart aristocracy of the Napoleonic First and Third
Empires. Between these more recent aristocrats and the
increasingly prosperous and pushing middle class another
wide gap existed. In spite of the lack of an apex—a monarch
and a court to crown the edifice—the social trend was
upwards ; everyone who was anyone was on the move,
aspiring, nearly always successfully, to swell the original
family kernel of wealth, position, power. Servants were
plentiful and cheap.. Social display was still elegant and
luxurious, sometimes fantastically so. The " lower classes "
—shopkeepers, industrial workers, farmers, and peasants,
were still a mere vulgar herd of small fry ; nobodies, despised
and ignored socially and on the whole, politically.

One comparatively new feature of this scene was the fact
that certain prosperous, cultured, refined Jewish families

were beginning to be allowed to share the aspirations and ambitions of Gentile society, and were finding less and less difficulty in gaining the entrée to circles which had hitherto remained closed to them. Their sons became professional soldiers, successful barristers and doctors, even popular and socially eligible men-about-town and members of the Mecca of the *jeunesse dorée*, the Jockey Club ; like the broker's son, Charles Haas, on whose elegant model Proust was to fashion the unforgettable character of Charles Swann. The Jews had, of course, for a long time past been the bankers of Royalty, of the aristocracy, of the State ; the providers of credit, the guardians and increasers of wealth. At the end of the nineteenth and the beginning of the twentieth centuries, when the banker was possibly the most important and powerful figure behind the scenes, he and his heir—more especially his heiress—began to be pleasantly received in the drawing-rooms of his clients, even in the most exclusive social circles.

Marcel Proust was Jewish only on his mother's side. The family were more than comfortably off, living in solid, though unostentatious, circumstances. On his father's side, included in his paternal heritage, Marcel had the taste, the respect, the almost instinctive small-town Frenchman's admiration for the local grandees ; an attitude similar to the English yeoman's pride in the county family, the occupants of the Big House, under whose shadow and protection he was born and reared. Marcel's romantic historical sense was an intellectual offshoot of this natural, unselfconscious traditionalism. From his mother's Jewish side he may have acquired an inferiority complex which urged him forward, as a similar driving-force may have urged Charles Haas forward, into the exclusive social world to which, until very recently, members of his race could never have aspired. Marcel's admiration for Haas—whom, when still an adolescent, he had one evening seen, but not dared speak to, at a dinner-party—inspired the first volume of his great novel, entitled *Du Côté de Chez Swann*. Years later he was to write : " And yet, dear Charles Haas, whom I knew when I was still a mere youth, and you were almost in your grave, it may be because the boy you probably thought a little fool made of you the hero of one of his novels, that one day the world will begin to talk of you again, and so you will continue to live "—a most accurate prophecy. But in real life as well as in his creative imagination, Marcel was profoundly affected by Haas. For Haas was the supremely successful Jewish social favourite, darling of fashionable ladies, dilettante, connoisseur, that Marcel himself aspired to be, and also in due course became. What Haas had achieved, Marcel set himself to achieve too, and maybe to surpass, quite apart from the literary interest he may have found in this typical man of the period.

In these two strains, in their intertwining and comingling— French traditionalism and Jewish inferiority complex—one must look for the sources of Proust's social opportunism and careerism.

Marcel had an excellent education and was a talented pupil. But even as a schoolboy he began to lay the foundations of his social career. One of his most intimate friends was Jacques Bizet, the son of the great composer, whose mother, a beauty, married after Bizet's early death a wealthy M. Straus. It was in the salon of Mme Straus that the young Marcel, as charming and naïf as Mozart's Cherubino, made his social début. For the rest of their lives he remained Geneviève Straus's devoted admirer. His success, as a youth-about-town, was rapid and widespread. His delicate good looks, his " amusingness," kindness and generosity towards his friends, won him admirers very quickly. He soon became the darling and favourite of many other ladies who ran literary or social salons. Though delicate and effeminate physically, he was exceptionally quick-witted and intelligent ; his dark eyes were meltingly expressive, his smile revealed dazzlingly white teeth. There are two delightful portraits of Marcel as a young man in *The Last Salon : Anatole France and his Muse*, by Mme Jeanne Maurice Pouquet. Mme Pouquet's first husband was Gaston de Caillavet, the well-known French playwright, and son of Mme Arman de Caillavet, the friend and inspirer of the great French novelist Anatole France. Gaston was another school-friend of Marcel's, who soon became a protégé of his mother's.

At the time of which Mme Pouquet writes, Marcel was doing his military service at Orleans, although, owing to his hay fever, he was excused most of the rougher activities of military training. He used to come to Paris on leave.

The frequenters of Mme Arman de Caillavet's salon saw Marcel very often on Sundays that year, crammed into his tight uniform, his head thrown back and hanging over one shoulder, sitting, almost lying, in one of the deep bergères, whose overflowing cushions made his warlike dress seem absurd. He used always to sink into a heap in his chair, as if overcome by a perpetual lassitude, which the future proved, alas, not to be a mere pose. He was always weighed down by a great fatigue. Although his face was serious, and his great brown eyes were melancholy, his very white teeth lit up his pale countenance, and his laughter broke forth on the slightest pretext. He was handsome, charming, and nice. This last epithet, which he used so often himself, best describes his character, his ways, his manner, his greeting, his willingness, and his friendship. Everything in him was nice. How good, how sensitive, he was ! How grateful for the slightest service, the tiniest attention ! And how frightfully and unreasonably sad he would become, if he were hurt, or if he thought he had reason to feel hurt !

Towards six o'clock on these wonderful Sundays the young soldier would be stuffed with sandwiches and cakes and given others to eat " on the trip." Nothing was more comical than to see Marcel making his farewells around the salon, embarrassed in his movements by his military cape and his little packages, with Gaston hustling him along so that he might not miss his train.

And another youthful portrait of him by Mme Pouquet is worth quoting. For it shows him in an environment which seems like a pre-view of some of the idyllic scenes in *A l'Ombre des Jeunes Filles en Fleurs*.

After finishing his military service, Marcel began to join Gaston and his friends at their tennis courts at Neuilly. He was not allowed to play so strenuous a game, but he would come to chat, and the girls and their mothers who sat around him in a circle under the sparse leaves, would listen devoutly to all he said.

It was he who brought their refreshments ; he would always arrive with a huge box of dainty things to eat. If it was hot, he was sent to a neighbouring shop for beer and lemonade, and he would come back panting under the burden of an appalling basket borrowed from the shopkeeper. Occasionally a ball would land in the midst of the conversation and the cakes ; the girls and the glasses would tremble, and Marcel would always accuse the players of aiming their shots " with malice aforethought." There may even have been a little malice in the shots, quite unknown to the players. Marcel's charm, and the tenderness that emanated from him and that he inspired in others, often irritated his comrades. They were a little jealous of it, and without any well-defined or disagreeable intention, they were not at all displeased to upset the " court of love " a little. This was the name they gave the chattering circle when they were in a poetic vein. When the game was ended, they came quickly over, to rest

" in the shade of the blossoming girls " and to enjoy with
them Marcel's agreeable chatter.   Many years afterwards,
à propos of a book he was writing, these memories of youth
returned to him, and he wrote to Mme Gaston de Caillavet :
" You will see blended into it something of the emotion I felt
in those days when I wondered if you were to be at the tennis
courts."

This youthful passion of Marcel's for Jeanne Pouquet was,
like all his emotions and relationships, from adolescence until
the very end of his life, not so simple and straightforward as
it seemed.   Undoubtedly it contained an element of sincere
admiration and devotion.   But, viewed in the light of our
knowledge of other aspects of his emotional life, it takes on
a slightly different complexion.   Marcel went out of his way
to underline his adoration of Jeanne, to such an extent that
Gaston, her fiancé, and his intimate friend, was roused to
jealousy.   But not for long, and there was indeed no cause
for it.   The truth was that Marcel already knew the true
trend of his emotional life, which was homosexual.   He
never hid this knowledge from himself, nor from those of
a similar disposition whom he could trust not to betray
him.   But it filled him with a sense of guilt, and required
unceasing vigilance and constant camouflage, lest it be
suspected by others ; above all others, by his mother, with
whom his relationship was one of the closest and most
constant intimacy.   During her entire lifetime he provided
himself with alibi after alibi, in the form of " hopeless "
passions for young girls or married women.   The girls were
always engaged to someone else, the married women were
chaste.

A clue to the other side of Marcel's nature exists in the
dedication of his first book, *Les Plaisirs et les Jours*, published
in 1896, when the author was twenty-five years old.   He had
always intended to become a writer, but twenty years were to

pass between the publication of this first youthful effort and the great work of his life. Yet even in adolescence he aspired to literary as well as social success. At the time of the publication of *les Plaisirs et les Jours* Marcel was a member of a small and rather smart literary group that founded a pretentious little review called *Le Banquet*. Among its members were Fernand Gregh, Henri Barbusse, Robert de Flers, and others who later became distinguished men of letters. Proust was regarded by his contemporaries as a light-weight, a feather-weight even, no more than a drawing-room littérateur, whose speciality was to be, for many years, the contribution of social notes and reportage to *Le Figaro*.

Les Plaisirs et les Jours was published with a preface by Anatole France, which his friend, Madame Arman de Caillavet, persuaded him to write for this first effort of Gaston's and her charming Marcel. The book was pretentiously got up—too much so even for the late nineties—with reproductions of flower-paintings by another of Marcel's women friends, the artist Madeleine Lemaire, and four compositions for the piano by his life-long friend the composer Reynaldo Hahn, who is nowadays best known for some exquisite song-settings. In spite of France's laudatory preface, Marcel's little essays and stories were received with almost no enthusiasm. I think the contemporary verdict in this case was singularly short-sighted and I shall deal with the contents of *Les Plaisirs et les Jours* in detail later on. I need only say here that they foreshadowed the style and in many respects the material of *A La Recherche du Temps Perdu* as clearly as the rosebud indicates the shape, texture, and perfume of the fully expanded flower.

But here let us glance at the dedication only. It was inscribed " To my friend Willie Heath, who died in Paris on October 3rd, 1893." Willie Heath was a young Scotsman

of Marcel's own age.   Here is the author's description of
him :

> It was in the Bois that I used often to meet you in the
> morning, having seen me coming, and waiting for me under
> the trees, standing there, resting, and similar to one of those
> young lords painted by Van Dyck, whose pensive elegance
> you shared.   In fact their elegance, like yours, was less a
> matter of dress than of the body, and their very bodies seemed
> to have received it and to continue to receive it from the
> soul : it is a moral elegance.   Everything contributed to
> accentuate this melancholy resemblance, even the background
> of branches in whose shade Van Dyck so often stayed the
> promenade of a king ; like so many of those who were his
> models, you also were soon to die, and in your eyes, as in
> theirs, one saw alternately the shadows of presentiment and
> the soft light of resignation.   But if the gracefulness of your
> pride belonged by right to the art of a Van Dyck, you derived
> rather more from Vinci through the mysterious intensity of
> your spiritual life.   Often, your finger raised, your eyes
> impenetrable and smiling in the face of the enigma which
> you would not disclose, you appeared to me like the Saint
> John the Baptist by Lionardo.   At that time we formed the
> dream, almost the plan, of living more and more with one
> another, in a circle of magnanimous and chosen women and
> men, far enough from stupidity, vice, and wickedness to feel
> ourselves sheltered from their vulgar barbs.

After a few more lines in this vein, there follows an
autobiographical reminiscence of considerable interest.

> When I was a very little child, the fate of no other Biblical
> personage seemed to me as miserable as that of Noah, because
> of the deluge, which kept him shut up in the Ark for forty
> days.   Later, I was often ill, and for many long days I, too,
> remained " in the ark."   I then understood that Noah had
> never seen the world so well as from the Ark, even although

it was shut and it was night on earth. When my convalescence
began, my mother, who had not left me and even at night
stayed with me, "opened the door of the Ark" and went
out. However, like the dove, she "returned the same
evening." Then I was cured, and like the dove, "she did not
come back." One had to start to live again, to turn outwards
from oneself, to hear harder words than those of my mother ;
even worse, hers, so perpetually sweet until then, were no
longer the same, but stamped with the severity of the life
and the duty which she had to teach me. Sweetness of the
suspension of living, of the true "Truce of God" which
stopped work and evil desires. "Grace" of illness, which
brings us close to those realities beyond death—and its graces
too, the graces from "those vain ornaments and those heavy
veils," gentle faithfulness of a mother and of a friend which
so often seemed like the very face of our own sorrow or like
the protective gesture our weakness implored, but which
stopped on the threshold of convalescence, often I suffered to
feel you so far from me, all you exiled descendants of the
dove of the Ark. And who, dear Willie, has not known
those moments when one wanted to be where you are ?

And a further important sidelight follows in the final
paragraph :

I give you this book. You are, alas, the only one of my
friends whose criticisms it does not have to fear. I am at
least confident that you would not have been shocked by its
freedom of tone. I have never pictured immorality except
in those of a delicate conscience. Too feeble to desire the
good, too noble fully to enjoy evil, knowing only suffering,
I have only been able to speak of them with enough pity to
purify these little sketches.

Apart from the two women by whom Proust's life was
permanently dominated—his mother and, after her death, his
housekeeper, Céleste Albaret, part model for the unforgettable

Françoise of his novel—he had many successful friendships
with women. He had a particular affinity with them, a
capacity for understanding, analysing, and describing feminine
psychology from, as it were, "within." Whether they
understood him as well as he understood them is, I think,
doubtful. One of Proust's feminine characteristics was a
feline love of gossip. He had a keen sense of humour,
particularly of the ridiculous, and is said to have been a
marvellous mimic. He also had his full share of the
fashionable Parisian's malice. All these qualities, which on
the surface appeared so frivolous, were later turned to
dazzling account in his great work. But long before he
began it they found vent in his conversation and in his
correspondence. His letters sometimes have a striking
vividness :

> By the way [he wrote to Mme Gaston de Caillavet], you
> may not have heard what Mme S—— said to the other lady.
> The other one, plagiarising Mme Récamier's (?) remark, said
> that she would know she was no longer beautiful when the
> little chimney-sweeps no longer turned to look as she passed.
> Mme S—— replied, " Oh, have no fear, my dear. So long
> as you dress the way you do, people will always turn to look
> after you ! "
> You probably know also of the letter Montesquiou wrote
> to Maurice de R——, of whom he had asked the loan of
> jewellery for a costume ball and who sent him only one tiny
> brooch, cautioning him not to lose it because it was a family
> jewel : " I was not aware that you had a family, but I did
> think you had jewelry." I am compensating myself for
> months of solitude and sadness by a quarter of an hour of
> frivolity with you, but I am afraid you will think my frivolity
> excessive.

For the reverse side of his malice was his occasionally
abject humility. Hypersensitive himself, and quick to take

umbrage at even an imagined slight, he was always fearful of hurting others. This morbid humility of his was allied to a habit of pressing the most expensive and exquisite presents on his friends, as if they had to be rewarded with almost Oriental lavishness for condescending to endure his affection.

The Montesquiou referred to in this letter was the celebrated Robert de Montesquiou, the dictator of the fashionable Paris of his day, with whom the only comparable individual is the English Beau Brummel. Marcel attached himself to this ambiguous figure with almost limpet-like persistence, and for years used him as his social guide and mentor and at the same time as a model, to be studied inwardly and outwardly with the most intense concentration, and on whom he was later partly to base his most magnificent and sinister character, the Baron de Charlus.

He was, however, on terms of friendship with many of his contemporaries whose lives and interests were of less restricted and exotic kind than those of Montesquiou.

In those days Marcel's chief claim to consideration as a serious writer lay in his detailed studies and translations of the works of Ruskin, at that time as fashionable in certain narrow French circles as in English ones. However, it was a slender enough claim, in itself, and a mere alibi for work. His father had hoped he would enter the diplomatic service, but Marcel had no bent for it. Various other professions were considered : the law, medicine. But nothing came of any of these suggestions. His chronic ill-health, his " attacks," his crises, asthma and hay fever became more frequent and more intense as he grew into maturity and barred the way to any serious profession. There was one to which he did indeed aspire ; with all his mind and all his emotional ardour he longed to be a writer, a professional and a great writer. But until he was thirty-four years of age he did not begin to be one.

Professor Proust died in 1903, leaving his family with ample means. Marcel had never left home, and he continued to reside there with his mother after his father's death. From his earliest childhood Mme Proust had dedicated her life to the care of her delicate elder son ; she had no other interests, and rarely went out ; but when Marcel entertained his brilliant friends at home she was too shy to appear except rarely and for a very short time.

Marcel was still relatively young when he began to acquire the peculiar manner of living which rightly gave him the reputation of an eccentric. Many of his friends refused to take his physical ill-health seriously, and considered that his chief ailment was hypochondria. Whether this was or was not the cause, the effect was that he was certainly ill. He arranged his whole life around his peculiar condition. As he was convinced that his asthma and hay fever were worse in the day-time, and because as a child he had suffered agonies from night-terrors and claustrophobia, he spent most of the early hours of the day in bed, and did not get up, generally, until late in the afternoon, or, frequently, in the evening. As he grew older, these habits became fixed. He would visit his friends at impossible hours, preferably after midnight, or send for them to visit him. At dawn they would depart, and he would return to bed, to sleep or write. The room in which he lived and worked became legendary. It was lined from ceiling to floor with cork, to keep out all irrelevant sounds and draughts. The windows were tightly shut, in order that no particle of pollen-laden dust should penetrate to it ; the suffocating atmosphere was impregnated with the odours of his constant " fumigations." When his women friends visited him Céleste Albaret made sure, before admitting them, that they wore neither fresh flowers nor even a drop of synthetic perfume. On the increasingly rare occasions when he left Paris to visit the country, to see once again the flowering hawthorns and apple-blossom orchards he adored, he travelled in a taxi and peered at the flowers through the closely sealed windows, with eyes drowned in tears of longing and self-pity.

Madame Proust died in 1905. Not until after her death, in 1906, was Marcel able at last to settle down to compose his vast masterpiece, *A La Recherche du Temps Perdu*. He had been making notes and sketches for it over a long time previously, but now he withdrew himself almost completely from the world and wrote feverishly. The cork-lined room was the centre of his apartment in the Boulevard Haussman, out of which he rarely stirred. He was oblivious to his surroundings but cherished this " home " because his mother had known it, and he could imagine her there. After some years, however, the building was sold to a commercial firm and he had to go. The removal was a calvary to him. According to one of his most devoted biographers, Léon-Pierre-Quint, he " emigrated lamentably." He finally landed in a dark furnished flat on the fourth floor of a house in the Rue Hamelin. His own description of it gives the measure of his despair. " It costs 16.000 francs and looks like a servant's room." He did not expect to stay there long, so he left most of his furniture in store. The children of the neighbours above kept tramping overhead ; Marcel sent them presents of felt slippers ! Léon-Pierre-Quint continues :

> He hoped soon to move ; he was simply camping there. But he was never to leave this strange and hostile abode, where . . . he was deprived of his most cherished possessions. He never managed to get even his books out of store. In the salon, the chairs were covered with dust-cloths. In the middle of the floor stood a chandelier. He remained in bed for longer and longer periods ; the bed was never made. Medicine bottles and empty jars were everywhere, mixed up with masses of papers. Old newspapers littered the floor

Amongst all this appalling disorder were the twenty large notebooks, piled on a table, which contained the last instalments of his work. . . . His illness was getting progressively worse ; he was in a constant fever. Sleep had left him, and he took every sort of drug to obtain it. Veronal made him sleep for three whole days. Then again, by taking stimulants, he remained awake for three days, working incessantly.

He went to bed, and got up, with all his clothes on, including several mufflers and mittens, for his circulation was ebbing and he was forever cold. But suddenly, in the middle of the night, he would get up, and clutching a mass of printer's proofs, he would arrive, a strange and almost unbelievable apparition, at his old haunt, the Ritz Hotel. There, huddled up in a fur coat, wraps and mufflers, he would instal himself for a few hours in the porter's lodge, " in this warm glass cage, where his mind was stimulated by watching the people coming in or going out of the hotel," and would sit there, correcting his proof sheets, scribbling, scribbling. . . .

A month before he died he wrote to some of his friends, telling them he was at last " leaving, definitely." " And then," he added, " it will really be ' Time Regained.' " Finally he developed pneumonia. He had for years, with a frenzied hatred of doctors, barricaded his door against any member of the medical profession. Even his brother, Dr. Robert Proust, dared not pass his threshold. At last, in a final attempt to save Marcel's life, he forced his way in ; but he was even at this hour compelled to retreat before the dying man's rage. At the very end, the doctors gained admittance to him, but by then they could do nothing for him. Léon-Pierre-Quint adds that in spite of great physical suffering he remained conscious to the end ; and although he was no longer able to write, he dictated his impressions on the subject of approaching death. He died on 18

November 1922. And in a way his death was a triumph. By sheer force of will-power he had postponed it until he had finished *A La Recherche du Temps Perdu*, and although he did not live to see the publication of the later volumes, he had no doubts as to his future fame. He did not believe in the immortality of the soul. But of his literary immortality he was serenely and justly confident.

CHAPTER II

IN SEARCH OF TIME LOST

MARCEL PROUST'S fame rests upon one work alone. In form and content this is unique, and likely to remain so. Both his method of approach and his style were alien to the past conventions of French literature, to the classical and orderly progression of the novel until his time. Partly for these reasons, *A La Recherche du Temps Perdu* found at first only a few admirers. Those who recognised it immediately, on the publication of the initial volumes, *Du Côté de Chez Swann*, for the work of genius it was, did not hesitate to proclaim their enthusiasm. But it was only slowly and gradually as succeeding volumes appeared at protracted intervals, over a period of thirteen years, that the whole vast plan, the immensely long and complicated story, the intricate ramifications of the design, became clear. For the work was conceived and carried out on a huge scale. It comprises sixteen volumes, several million words, and a whole world of characters.

Proust began to write it around 1906 and had finished all but the final proof corrections of the last volume just before his death in 1922. The order of publication was as intermittent as the progression of the inter-linked stories of the various characters. As will be seen from the following chronology, there was an interval of five years between the appearance of *Du Côté de Chez Swann* and *A l'Ombre des Jeunes Filles en Fleurs*, whilst the subsequent volumes were published at intervals of between two and three years. At Proust's death, in 1922, *La Prisonnière*, *Albertine Disparue*, and *Le Temps Retrouvé* were still in manuscript. *A l'Ombre des Jeunes Filles en Fleurs* received the Prix Goncourt in 1918, against considerable opposition from those who considered that a simultaneously published war novel had far greater and more topical claims to it.

A La Recherche du Temps Perdu is not organised according to any conventional literary principle. In the strict sense, in outward progression, it has neither " a beginning, a middle," nor " an end." In fact what, for the reader, is " the end " was, for the author, a beginning. It does not appear to be founded on any logical or rational plan. There is, indeed, a plan, a very definite plan. But the impetus which gave birth to it was a mystical one ; it was conceived in the author's subconscious mind, and he fashioned it accordingly, as he was moved to do, by the erratic, intermittent impulses which brought back the recollections and the re-living of his past into his conscious memory, and in doing so, stirred his creative powers to action.

Before discussing *A La Recherche du Temps Perdu* in further detail, I have tried to give here, first, a bare and very condensed summary of the story. For, without some such superficial guide, it might be impossible to follow the subsequent discussion of its incomparably rich and diverse ramifications. In this résumé I have left out all but the most essential incidents and the leading characters. It should be regarded merely as a kind of simplified railway guide to the journey through Proust's country, but in no sense as an indicator to the natural, archæological, historical and artistic treasures to be discovered there.

However, it should be possible for the reader, using this rough indicator, to " dip " into any volume of *A La Recherche du Temps Perdu* provided with the essential knowledge of the background events.

The dates in brackets, after the titles of the respective
volumes, refer to the years of their publication.

1. *Du Côté de Chez Swann*. I and II. (Published 1913)

The narrator, as a small boy living with his parents in
Paris, spends his holidays at his grandfather's house in
the small provincial town of Combray, with his grand-
parents, parents, Aunt Léonie and her cook-housekeeper,
Françoise, who later becomes his parents' and then his own
servant. He suffers from night-terrors, and when he is put
to bed cannot sleep until his mother has come to comfort
him. On the occasion when the story opens, he waits for
the sound of the little bell on the garden gate, which tells
him that the visitor his parents have been entertaining,
M. Charles Swann, is at last leaving, and that his mother
will soon, now, come up to him. The family take their
walks "*du Côté de chez Swann*," along the banks of the
river Vivonne, where the rich M. Swann has his country
seat, Tansonville. But they never call on him there, because
he has married his former mistress, Odette de Crécy, whom
the respectable provincial bourgeoisie do not receive socially.
The Swanns have a small girl, Gilberte, whom Marcel
glimpses through the gates one day, together with her mother,
and a strange-looking middle-aged man, who later turns out
to have been the Baron de Charlus, the notorious aristocrat,
and member of the ducal family of Guermantes, the local
grandees. In the church at Combray Marcel first sees the
reigning lovely young Duchesse de Guermantes. Another
important neighbour is the great but still not famous composer
Vinteuil, whose daughter is a notorious Lesbian.

The second volume (entitled *Un Amour de Swann*) tells the
story of Swann's passion for the lady of easy virtue, Odette
de Crécy. She introduces him to her friends M. and Madame

Verdurin, rich and vulgar but cultured middle-class patrons
of minor intellectuals and artists. Odette is unfaithful to
Swann with the Comte de Forcheville, but although he knows
this his desire for her is so consuming that he pays her own
price for her " favours "—marriage.

2. *A l'Ombre des Jeunes Filles en Fleurs.* I and II. (1918)

The narrator, now a youth, spends a holiday with his
grandmother at the seaside town of Balbec, in Normandy.
Here, at the Grand Hotel, they meet his grandmother's old
convent-school friend, the aristocratic Mme de Villeparisis, of
the feudal house of Guermantes, whose relations, however,
disapprove of her for having been for many years the mistress
of the diplomat, M. de Norpois. Mme de Villeparisis is
visited by her handsome great nephew, another Guermantes,
Robert de Saint-Loup, who is doing his military service in
the nearby garrison town of Doncières. Marcel and Robert
become intimate friends. Robert is in love with a Jewish
girl, Rachel, who has been in a house of ill-fame, but has
ambitions to become an actress. Also at Balbec, Marcel meets
for the first time Robert's uncle, the extraordinary Baron de
Charlus, the younger brother of the Duc de Guermantes.
He is mystified by de Charlus's strange alternations of
friendliness and contemptuousness towards himself. He is
strongly attracted by a group of gay and laughing girls and
falls in love with one of them (he had previously been in
love with Swann's daughter, Gilberte). Her name is
Albertine, and she is an orphan, of obscure social background.

3. *Du Côté de Guermantes.* I and II. (1921)

Marcel's parents rent an apartment in the town residence
of the Duc de Guermantes. Marcel has been dreaming of

the Duchesse, in the light of her historically glamorous family tradition, ever since his childhood in Combray ; now that he sees her constantly he imagines himself in love with her. She is an acknowledged leader of the Faubourg Saint-Germain. The youth's one ambition is to meet the Duchesse, socially, and in this he at last succeeds when she comes to a tea-party given by Mme de Villeparisis, and he is introduced to her. Marcel's grandmother is dying, and the Duc de Guermantes pays a formal call of sympathy. After her death, Marcel's mother goes to stay at Combray, leaving him alone in their apartment, under the care of Françoise. Albertine comes to visit him, and they lie down side by side on his bed. Dusk falls, Françoise comes in with a lamp, and is shocked to find them together. She suspects that Albertine has designs on her young master, and becomes her implacable enemy. Marcel meets Swann at the Guermantes'. He is dying and has come to pay them a farewell visit, but neither the Duc nor the Duchesse, about to leave for a dinner-party, will admit that their old friend is calling on them for the last time.

4. *Sodome et Gomorrhe.* I, II, and III. (1921)

This opens with a detailed analysis of homosexuality which, at the time of publication, caused a sensation. The narrator watches the fertilisation of a rare flower by a bumble-bee, its only suitable " mate," and, soon afterwards, the first meeting between the Baron de Charlus and the tailor, Jupien, who has a lock-up shop in the courtyard of the Guermantes mansion. Marcel is at last invited to a reception by the Princesse de Guermantes. In the course of a conversation at this party with Robert de Saint-Loup, a new character is " planted," the chambermaid of a Mme Putbus, whom Robert tells Marcel he has met in a brothel. This woman is

a Lesbian, and although she is only introduced obliquely and
never appears in the story except by indirect reference, she
figures prominently in the next two volumes in Marcel's
speculations about Albertine's secret life.   At the same party
Marcel again meets de Charlus, but now that he has discovered
that the hitherto enigmatic Baron is homosexual, he finds
himself no longer puzzled by his behaviour towards himself.
After the party, Albertine visits him again and the relationship
between them develops further.   But he does not see her
again until after the death of his grandmother, when he goes
for a second time to Balbec, attended by Françoise.   He now
begins to realise that he is in love with Albertine, and enters
on the calvary this love is to mean to him.   He takes her to
dinner with the Verdurins, at their magnificent country
estate, La Raspelière.   He discovers in conversation with her
that Albertine has known the notorious daughter of the
composer Vinteuil, and his suspicion that she is a Lesbian
tortures him.   In the train, on the way to the Verdurins,
they meet de Charlus, on a station platform.   For the first
time the Baron sees, on the opposite platform, the young
violinist Morel.   The passion of de Charlus for Morel now
becomes a secondary theme, complementary to the story of
Marcel's affair with Albertine.   Through Morel, de Charlus
becomes a member of Mme Verdurin's " little clan," but
makes no attempt to conceal his disdain for her and her
sycophants.   Marcel's mother is alarmed by the thought that
he may want to marry Albertine, who is socially a nobody ;
he assures her that he has no such intention, but persuades her
to invite Albertine to come and stay with them in their Paris
apartment.

5. *La Prisonnière*.   I and II.   (1924)

Albertine is living in Marcel's home.   He is perpetually
ravaged by jealousy of her secret life.   He tries to bind her

to him by every device he can use ; to escape his surveillance
for short periods, she tells him involved and complicated lies.
Their life together is a battle : on his side to bind her to him
more securely and irrevocably ; on hers, to escape the toils,
without having to sacrifice the advantages he gives her,
money, clothes, jewels, etc., and the tenuous but alluring
prospect of a good match with the wealthy young man.

The narrator describes the death of Bergotte, the great
writer, and in this description adumbrates for the first time
his theories of life and death, Time and Eternity.

In order to launch Morel socially and professionally,
M. de Charlus collaborates with Mme Verdurin in giving a
musical party. On this occasion he insults her as never
before. He has invited all the leading aristocratic personages
of his acquaintance, and as they arrive, he receives them, but
pointedly omits to introduce Mme Verdurin to them. After
the party, she takes a terrible revenge. She and her husband
inform Morel that de Charlus is wanted by the police on
account of his life of homosexual vice. Morel, himself a
young scoundrel, is terrified of the scandal that might break
him as well, and, worked on by the Verdurins, publicly
repudiates de Charlus. Their affair is at an end ; the Baron
becomes seriously ill.

Marcel continues to keep Albertine in his apartment. He
never allows her to go out at night. Their fencing match
continues : he, forever trying to discover her secrets, she,
lying to defend them. " Our life together, when I was not
jealous, was one long boredom, and when I was jealous, one
long misery. Even had it been possible for me to be happy
with her, it could not have lasted." Whenever he feels
particularly uncertain of her, he too lies, suggesting to her
that he has tired of her, and that she should leave him. By
such pretences he hopes to retain her. Finally he decides
that he really is bored with her, and begins to contemplate

a trip to Venice. One morning he wakes up, determined to
go there. He rings for Françoise, to bring him a time-table.
But when Françoise comes in, she tells him : " Miss Albertine
left this morning, at nine o'clock. I gave her a lecture, and
insisted she should wait until Monsieur awoke, but she
wouldn't. She gave me this letter for you."

6. *Albertine Disparue.* I and II. (1926)

Marcel is in despair. He sends Robert de Saint-Loup to
Albertine's aunt, in Touraine, with a present of 30,000 francs
towards her husband's election expenses, ostensibly from a
friend who is engaged to Albertine. If she does not return,
their engagement will be broken. Saint-Loup undertakes the
mission, incidentally informing Marcel that he also is thinking
of marrying, but without mentioning the name of his future
bride. Marcel, not wanting Albertine to guess how madly
he wants her to return, writes to ask her advice as to whether
he should invite her friend, Andrée, to stay with him. His
mind is entirely preoccupied with his jealousy, which he
analyses in all its phases. He foresees that a time will come
when he will no longer suffer through his love for Albertine,
which will die, just as his passion for Swann's daughter,
Gilberte, his adoration of the Duchesse de Guermantes, and
his great love for his grandmother, have already been outlived.
But he still loves Albertine, and finally sends her a telegram,
imploring her to return to him on her own conditions. But
she never returns. Instead, he receives a telegram from her
aunt, Mme Bontemps, informing him that Albertine has
been killed in a riding accident. He is, of course, completely
prostrated. But now his jealousy of her secret life, of which
she herself will nevermore give him the explanation, takes a
posthumous turn. He gets in touch with everyone, anyone,
who could have known her secrets. He never succeeds in

meeting anybody with whom she might have had a love affair or a liaison, but there is indirect evidence to suggest that she was, in fact, a Lesbian.

At last he feels with mingled relief and regret that his passion for Albertine is beginning to fade, and that he will soon be able to be interested in other women once again. As he calls at the Guermantes residence, he meets three young girls just leaving it, of whom one, a pretty little reddish blonde, looks at him with special interest. He goes to call on the Duc and Duchesse, and discovers that this girl is Gilberte Swann, his first love. Poor Swann is dead, and no one wants to remember him. The Duchesse had always refused to receive his daughter. But his widow, Odette, has married her former lover, the Count de Forcheville ; Gilberte has inherited a fortune from one of Swann's relatives, and has been adopted by de Forcheville. As she is now a great heiress she is received everywhere, although her father was a Jew and her mother a courtesan. Marcel is no longer in the least in love with her. He has a slight affair with Andrée, Albertine's friend, who confesses that she and Albertine had been lovers, and that Albertine did prefer women. She also explains Albertine's sudden departure : Mme Bontemps, wanting to get her off her hands, and fearing that Marcel would never marry her, had arranged another match for her. But these discoveries no longer cause him acute sorrow, only emotional fatigue; Albertine now means little or nothing to him.

He and his mother leave for Venice, which he has for so long wanted to visit. Here he receives a telegram : " My friend, you think I am dead, forgive me I am very much alive, I would like to see you, discuss marriage with you, when do you return ? Tenderly. ALBERTINE." But he feels no pleasure in this sudden revival. The telegram, however, turns out to have been from Gilberte. Albertine really is dead. He is about to leave Venice, and in the train,

reading his mail, he discovers the amazing fact that Robert
de Saint-Loup and Gilberte Swann are about to marry.
Apparently, in the highest social circles, nothing but money
counts any longer.

After their marriage, Gilberte invites Marcel to Tansonville,
Swann's country seat, where she is living. She tells him that
Robert is not only unfaithful to her, but has developed the
homosexual tastes of his uncle, de Charlus, and is having an
affair with the scoundrelly Morel. Gilberte is still attracted
by Marcel, but he no longer has any vestige of his former
love for her. On his walks he grieves to find that he cannot
relive his past at Combray ; nothing of his old self seems
to remain, not even his memories.

7. *Le Temps Retrouvé.* I and II. (1926)

There is a complete break between the final volume and
the rest. Years have elapsed—we are not told how many—
but the narrator has spent a long time in a nursing home.
The 1914–1918 war has broken out. On his return to Paris
the city is dark and deserted. Robert de Saint-Loup is at
the front, and is killed in action. M. Verdurin is dead ; Mme
Verdurin, with a large fortune, is queening it at the Hotel
Majestic. M. de Charlus is pro-German. The narrator, lost
one night in the dark streets of Paris, strays into a homosexual
brothel, kept by the former tailor, Jupien, for M. de Charlus's
vicious pleasures. Morel is a deserter. In due course the war
ends, but Marcel takes little interest in life ; he is now a
semi-invalid. However, he decides to go to a musical party
given by the Princesse de Guermantes—none other than the
widow Verdurin ! On the way he meets de Charlus, who
has had a stroke and is being looked after by Jupien.

As Marcel is about to enter the mansion, he bumps his
foot on a loose paving-stone. This tiny shock causes a tremor

of memory which develops when, in the library, he is awaiting the end of a musical performance before entering the salon. He realises, as he almost loses consciousness, owing to the overwhelming psychological experience he is having, that he has somehow found the key to unlock his memory, that he has discovered the way back to his old selves, regained Time Lost, and that he will now at last be able to write his novel.

In the salon he discovers that Time has altered all the social personalities whom he once knew. The Duc de Guermantes has become the lover of Mme de Forcheville, formerly Odette Swann ; the Duchesse the friend of the actress Rachel, Robert's former mistress. Finally, Gilberte introduces him to her sixteen-year-old daughter, child of the union of the Guermantes and Swann families. Through her dual ancestry, this young girl links up for Marcel all the various disparate threads that have been intertwined with his own experience.

Marcel has recaptured Time Lost, for which during so many sterile years he had been seeking. He begins at last to write his long novel. For Time Regained can now be tamed, subordinated to his memory and his creative will. He has found himself, and at the same moment, Eternity.

CHAPTER III

THE CHARACTERS

THE supreme test for the novelist lies in the problem of his characters. Only the greatest masters of the craft can create individuals who live in the memory, whom we recognise as true types, and know, sometimes more intimately and vividly than our own living acquaintances. Of the English master-novelists Dickens springs to mind in this connection as the most obvious example of a writer who lives less by and through his social theories and the powerful indignation with which he expressed them, hardly at all by his " plots " which were often hackneyed and slip-shod, but almost solely by the splendour of his characters—Micawber, Fagin, Pecksniff, and the rest. And it is important to note, for the purpose of comparison with Proust, that the most memorable Dickens characters are by no means the most sympathetic. The odious Uriah Heep (what genius in that name !) remains far more firmly in the reader's memory than any of the author's saccharine heroines.

I remember H. G. Wells—who also created living and unforgettable characters in Kipps and Mr. Polly—at a dinner-party he once gave at his flat in Paris, challenging my enthusiasm for Proust the novelist, on the ground that he was "a mere snob." H. G., in spite of his immense talent, the colossal vitality of his imagination and grasp of form, was, nevertheless (as Lenin so woundingly pointed out after their unsuccessful meeting), a late nineteenth-century petit bourgeois ; with his ingenuous non-dialectical materialism, his passion for science, which was supposed to have all the

answers to metaphysical and social as well as biological and
physical problems, his contempt for " beautay " and culture.
Although he lived for many years in France he spoke the
language haltingly, with the accent of the English schoolboy.
He admitted that to read Proust in the original was beyond
him.   He knew him only in translation, which, even as
faithful as Scott-Moncrieff's version, can yet never hope to
give the full flavour, the entire essence, the shades and subtleties
of meaning of the Proustian style.

But is it perhaps not characteristic of most middle-class
persons, whether big or little bourgeois, whether great
novelists or not, to be snobs ? Not only was Wells himself
also a snob—he adored " great ladies," for example, even
if they were only the relicts of obscure or wealthy knights or
baronets—but some of our greatest English writers have been
as much accused of this vice as Marcel Proust.   Jane Austen
and Thackeray immediately spring to mind.   Yet who is to
draw the line between snobbery and satire, between a realistic
apprehension of class distinction, when it is an accepted convention of the writer's period, and an analysis of the writer's
characters which, far from condoning this vice in them, holds
it up to the reader's ridicule and contempt ?

Whilst the social snobbery of Proust the man cannot be
ignored, Proust the author constantly and stingingly flayed
the snobbery of his characters ; most of whom were studied
from living models.   One can prove this conclusively by
quotation, but I will refrain from recalling more than a few
examples.

M. Legrandin, the bourgeois of Combray, who " cut "
Marcel's family after Mass ; his sister, the dim provincial
aristocrat, Madame de Cambremer, and her husband, the
stupid Marquis ; the pompous ex-Ambassador, M. de Norpois;
the vital and terrifying Madame Verdurin, with her despotic
rule over her " little clan," her furious denigration of all

those socially superior, who would not " receive " her ; her
envenomed hatred of the great and abominably proud aristocrat, M. de Charlus, who at one of the parties he had induced
her to give for his protégé, the violinist Morel, refused to
introduce her to his friends from the Faubourg Saint-Germain,
thereby incurring her terrible vengeance ; the disdainful,
inverted snobbery of his charming nephew, Robert de Saint-
Loup, who from a sort of social masochism deliberately chose
his lovers and friends from among his social inferiors ; the
crude intellectual snobbery of the middle-class Jew, Marcel's
school-friend Bloch ; even the most lovable character in his
enormous portrait gallery, his servant Françoise, does not
escape his derision. When Marcel's family rent an apartment
in the Guermantes mansion, Françoise quickly makes friends
with the ducal liverymen, and with relish repeats to her young
master their references to " our " impending visits to the
great country-houses which they and their masters frequented.

All these types of snobbery are unsparingly castigated. But
Proust's finest scorn is reserved for the Duc and Duchesse
de Guermantes ; the Duchesse, who refers to the Iéna's,
descended from the Napoleonic aristocracy, as " *ces gens au
nom d'un pont* " (" those people called after a bridge ").

Never has an author used more vitriolic irony than Proust,
in the scene in *Du Côté de Guermantes*, in which he describes
the visit of Swann, dying of cancer, to the Duc and Duchesse
de Guermantes, who are about to leave for a dinner-party.
The Duchesse wants Charles, a connoisseur of Italian art, to
accompany her to Italy in ten months' time.

> " Madame " [he answers], " I am really afraid that it will
> not be possible."   [The Duchesse continues to gossip with
> him . . .] " I should like to know, all the same," Mme de
> Guermantes asked him, " how, ten months before the time,
> you can tell that a thing will be impossible."   " My dear
> Duchess, I will tell you if you insist upon it, but, first of all,

you can see that I am very ill." "Yes, my little Charles, I
don't think you look at all well. I'm not pleased with your
colour, but I'm not asking you to come with me next week,
I ask you to come in ten months. In ten months one has time
to get oneself cured, you know." At this point a footman
came in to say that the carriage was at the door. "Come,
Oriane, to horse," said the Duke, already pawing the ground
with impatience as though he were himself one of the horses
that stood waiting outside. "Very well, give me in one
word the reason why you can't come to Italy," the Duchess
put it to Swann as she rose to say good-bye to us. "But,
my dear friend, it's because I shall then have been dead for
several months. According to the doctors I consulted last
winter, the thing I've got—which may, for that matter,
carry me off at any moment—won't in any case leave me
more than three or four months to live, and even that is a
generous estimate," replied Swann with a smile, while the
footman opened the glazed door of the hall to let the Duchess
out. "What's that you say?" cried the Duchess, stopping
for a moment on her way to the carriage, and raising her
fine eyes, their melancholy blue clouded by uncertainty.
Placed for the first time in her life between two duties as
incompatible as getting into her carriage to go out to dinner
and shewing pity for a man who was about to die, she could
find nothing in the code of conventions that indicated the
right line to follow, and, not knowing which to choose, felt
it better to make a show of not believing that the latter
alternative need be seriously considered, so as to follow the
first, which demanded of her at that moment less effort, and
thought that the best way of settling the conflict would be to
deny that any existed. "You're joking," she said to Swann.
"It would be a joke in charming taste," replied he, ironically.
"I don't know why I am telling you this; I have never said
a word to you before about my illness. But as you asked
me, and as now I may die at any moment. . . . But whatever
I do I mustn't make you late; you're dining out, remember,"
he added, because he knew that for other people their own

social obligations took precedence of the death of a friend,
and could put himself in her place by dint of his instinctive
politeness. But that of the Duchess enabled her also to
perceive in a vague way that the dinner to which she was
going must count for less to Swann than his own death. And
so, while continuing on her way towards the carriage, she
let her shoulders droop, saying : " Don't worry about our
dinner. It's not of any importance ! " But this put the
Duke in a bad humour, who exclaimed : " Come, Oriane,
don't stop there chattering like that and exchanging your
jeremiads with Swann ; you know very well that Mme de
Saint-Euverte insists on sitting down to table at eight o'clock
sharp. We must know what you propose to do ; the horses
have been waiting for a good five minutes. I beg your
pardon, Charles," he went on, turning to Swann, " but it's
ten minutes to eight already. Oriane is always late, and it
will take us more than five minutes to get to old Saint-
Euverte's."

Mme de Guermantes advanced resolutely towards the
carriage and uttered a last farewell to Swann. " You know,
we can talk about that another time ; I don't believe a word
you've been saying, but we must discuss it quietly. I expect
they gave you a dreadful fright ; come to luncheon, whatever
day you like " (with Mme de Guermantes things always
resolved themselves into luncheons), " you will let me know
your day and time," and, lifting her red skirt, she set her foot
on the step. She was just getting into the carriage when,
seeing this foot exposed, the Duke cried in a terrifying voice :
" Oriane, what have you been thinking of, you wretch ?
You've kept on your black shoes ! With a red dress ! Go
upstairs quick and put on red shoes, or rather," he said to
the footman, " tell the lady's maid at once to bring down
a pair of red shoes." " But, my dear," replied the Duchess
gently, annoyed to see that Swann, who was leaving the house
with me but had stood back to allow the carriage to pass out
in front of us, could hear, " since we are late." " No, no,
we have plenty of time. It is only ten to ; it won't take us

ten minutes to get to the Parc Monceau. And, after all,
what would it matter ? If we turned up at half-past eight
they'd have to wait for us, but you can't possibly go there in
a red dress and black shoes. Besides, we shan't be the last,
I can tell you ; the Sassenages are coming, and you know
they never arrive before twenty to nine." The Duchess
went up to her room. " Well," said M. de Guermantes to
Swann and myself, " we poor, down-trodden husbands,
people laugh at us, but we are of some use, all the same. But
for me, Oriane would have been going out to dinner in black
shoes." " It's not unbecoming," said Swann, " I noticed the
black shoes and they didn't offend me in the least." " I don't
say you're wrong," replied the Duke, " but it looks better to
have them to match the dress. Besides, you needn't worry,
she would no sooner have got there than she'd have noticed
them, and I should have been obliged to come home and
fetch the others. I should have had my dinner at nine o'clock.
Good-bye, my children," he said, thrusting us gently from
the door, " get away before Oriane comes down again. It's
not that she doesn't like seeing you both. On the contrary,
she's too fond of your company. If she finds you still here
she will start talking again, she is tired out already, she'll
reach the dinner-table quite dead. Besides, I tell you frankly,
I'm dying of hunger. I had a wretched luncheon this
morning, when I came from the train. There was a devil
of a *béarnaise* sauce, I admit, but in spite of that I shan't be
at all sorry, not at all sorry to sit down to dinner. Five
minutes to eight ! Oh, women, women ! She'll give us
both indigestion before to-morrow. She is not nearly as
strong as people think." The Duke felt no compunction at
speaking thus of his wife's ailments and his own to a dying
man, for the former interested him more, appeared to him
more important. And so it was simply from good breeding
and good fellowship that, after politely shewing us out, he
cried " from off stage," in a stentorian voice from the porch
to Swann, who was already in the courtyard : " You, now,
don't let yourself be taken in by the doctors' nonsense, damn

them. They're donkeys. You're as strong as the Pont Neuf. You'll live to bury us all ! " [1]

It is for the reader to judge whether that passage was written by a " mere snob " or by one of the greatest masters of the novel.

Even before the whole of *A La Recherche du Temps Perdu* had been published, one of Proust's admirers, M. François Fosca, planned to compile a " dictionary " or directory of the Proustian characters. The author was most interested in this plan, and wrote him a long letter, explaining his views on how his persons should be presented. And such a catalogue would be of great interest. For the Proustian world, like the Dickensian world, is stocked with human figures in greater numbers than the average reader can remember precisely, without mnemonic refreshment. Apart from the leading personages, there are dozens of minor ones, clearly sketched and mostly germane to the plot or the atmosphere at one point or another. Some of them are named, like Mlle de Stermaria, whom the author invites to a rendezvous, but who, to his despair, does not turn up. Others are known either by their first names or nicknames only, like the kitchen-maid, " the Charity of Giotto " ; some are anonymous, like the famous Lesbian chambermaid of Mme Putbus, who plays a pivotal part in Marcel's speculations on Albertine's secret life.

It is this wealth of human material, in addition to the wealth of descriptive background, that gives *A La Recherche du Temps Perdu* its imaginative richness and solidity.

Before discussing some of the principal characters individually, it may be helpful to attempt to group them semi-diagrammatically, according to their places in the general plan. This list is by no means complete, but includes the most important

[1] *The Guermantes Way*, vol. ii, pp. 391 *et seq.*

figures. We can classify them roughly in the three following divisions :

1. *THE NARRATOR, his Family, and Friends.*—These include his MOTHER, father, GRANDMOTHER, Uncle Alphonse, Aunt Léonie, and the family cook-housekeeper, FRANÇOISE. Their neighbours, M. Legrandin ; the composer Vinteuil, his daughter and her (anonymous) Lesbian girl-friend ; Marcel's school-friend, the young Jewish " intellectual " Bloch, his sisters and his uncle, M. Nissim Bernard ; the narrator's father's friend, the ex-Ambassador, M. de Norpois. In this group can also be included the staff of the Grand Hotel at Balbec, and, especially, the " blossoming girls "—Gisèle, Rosemonde, Andrée, and ALBERTINE, whom he meets at Balbec.

2. *The SWANN Circle.*—This comprises, first and foremost, CHARLES SWANN ; his mistress, later his wife, ODETTE DE CRÉCY ; their daughter, GILBERTE ; and the novelist, Bergotte. MME VERDURIN, Odette's rich middle-class friend ; M. Verdurin, and the members of Mme Verdurin's " little clan " ; " the faithful " as she calls them, including the painter, Elstir ; Dr. Cottard and his wife ; the philosopher Brichot ; and the artist, Ski ; the Count de Forcheville, Odette's lover and second husband.

3. *The GUERMANTES " Set."*—The Prince and Princesse de Guermantes-Bavière, the DUC and DUCHESSE DE GUER-MANTES ; the Duke's younger brother, PALAMÈDE, Baron de CHARLUS ; their sister, Mme de Marsantes ; her son, ROBERT DE SAINT-LOUP ; Mme de Villeparisis their aunt, and a host of minor relations and connections, genealogical and social, as well as certain European Royalties to whom they are distantly related. Among the " low-life " characters that belong on this side, the chief are RACHEL, Robert de Saint-Loup's mistress, JUPIEN, de Charlus's man, and MOREL, de Charlus's " protégé."

Looked at from one point of view, *A La Recherche du Temps Perdu* is a *roman à clef* in the classical French tradition. Ever since its appearance admirers of the work have been busily seeking for the "originals" of the characters. A celebrated demi-mondaine of the period, Laure Heyman, an old friend of Proust, when he sent her *Du Côté de Chez Swann*, was deeply offended by the resemblance she claimed existed between herself and Odette de Crécy. Marcel wrote at length to explain to her that there was none, nor had any resemblance been intended. The view has been widely expressed that the Baron de Charlus was a portrait of the famous social leader and dilettante littérateur of the period, an intimate friend of Proust, Robert de Montesquiou. Marcel owed de Montesquiou a very great deal, from social introductions to famous salons, to education in aesthetic appreciation. Montesquiou aspired to be recognised as a great poet and man of letters, but totally failed in this ambition. When, in their later years, Marcel's novel appeared, and the Prix Goncourt was awarded to *A L'Ombre des Jeunes Filles en Fleurs*, Montesquiou was miserably jealous of his young protégé's success. They had a honeyed and vinegary correspondence on the subject of the characters ; de Montesquiou claiming to recognise them, Proust explaining that not one of them was "taken from life" but that they were all composites, not individual portraits.

There is no space and it would be too complicated to go into this correspondence here, or into other such details. If —and this is admittedly not the case—*A La Recherche du Temps Perdu* were pure fiction from start to finish, it would still be a work of genius ; if it were not a masterpiece, the fact that many of its episodes may actually have occurred, or that most of the leading and several of the minor characters were partly taken from life, would have little importance.

Those readers, however, who are interested in the Proustian " Who's Who " are referred to *Robert de Montesquiou et Marcel Proust* (Flammarion, Paris, 1925) and *Marcel Proust* (Flammarion, Paris, 1948) by Mme Elisabeth de Gramont. Mme de Gramont, Duchesse de Clermont-Tonnerre, the distinguished French authoress, was for many years an intimate friend and admirer of Proust, and knew " everybody " in the Paris of his day. Her two books contain authoritative, and for the student of the details of his life and period, indispensable information on this aspect.

Proust's father was a medical practitioner with a scientific discipline and outlook. Marcel's paternal background provided him with a fair amount of biological instruction in addition to his education in the humanities and literature. It is clear that he had at least a superficial knowledge of biological laws and an avid interest in the subject. Again and again he goes to biology for his analogies. And in presenting his characters, he uses a twofold method. On the one hand, he sets them always in historical, genealogical perspective ; on the other, he places them almost, as it were, on a microscopic slide, for his own and the reader's easier analysis.

It is through this partly scientific, partly historical approach, that he invests them for us with that startling clarity, that liveliness, that makes most of his leading characters so completely rounded, so real, so human. Invariably, before they reveal themselves subjectively, they have been objectively studied, taken apart, probed, and put together again. Even including the mere " bit " and " crowd " players, not one of the characters concerned in the story, revealed in one episode or another, related to one group or coterie or another, fails to be presented to us neatly labelled and ticketed, complete with their respective genealogies ; whether these lead back to alliances among European Royal Houses four or five

centuries previously, as in the case of the Guermantes ; to
the rich soil of France and the peasant stock which bred
Françoise, or merely to the Stock Exchange, whence Charles
Swann's fortune was derived, or the slums of Paris that produced a Rachel, a Morel, or a Jupien. They are, one and all,
creatures of heredity and environment, as " closely conditioned," to use a biologist's phrase, by the past from which
they have emerged, as any " pure line " of mice or fruit-flies
in a scientific laboratory.

But if they are thus impressed with a quality of vividness
that stamps them indelibly on our memory, in another way
the Proustian characters are extraordinarily flat and puppet-
like. Conditioned by their pasts as they are, they seem
weighted down and chained to their circumstances, rarely if
ever capable of active psychological development, but merely
of passive evolution, according to the action and inter-action
on their minds of biological factors, such as ill-health or
advancing age, or environmental ones, such as social elevation
or decline. Every detail of their behaviour, whether actual
or potential, has been laid down from the beginning. None
of them ever changes, either for the better or the worse ;
all they do is gradually to unfold, to reveal themselves more
completely, as might a rose, from bud to overblown bloom,
or a cabbage, from seed to dinner-table. As the Duchesse
de Guermantes grows older, her pleasure in the society of
her social inferiors, formerly merely an elegant affectation,
becomes her sole distraction. Gilberte Swann-de Forcheville-
de Saint Loup, at first a vain, superficial, affected girl, though
no fool, in womanhood becomes a disillusioned bride, a bored
and embittered social climber. Robert de Saint-Loup, that
gallant young aristocrat, does not suddenly acquire, but merely
develops after his marriage to Gilberte, the latent homosexual
tastes which, like his uncle, de Charlus (who was also married
for several years) he has inherited ; presumably along with his

blue blood. Françoise does not change either, in the pattern (though later in the vocabulary) of her racy peasant utterances, or in her culinary talent, or in her possessive devotion to her master. Albertine retains her secret even after death.

The virtuosity with which Proust handled his material is demonstrated over and over again as the characters are introduced and gradually revealed. The best illustration of this point is probably de Charlus. We first see him through the eyes of Marcel the child, behind the gates of Tansonville, with Odette and Gilberte. Here he is presented as the middle-aged gentleman who, according to local gossip, is the lover of Mme Swann. He barely attracts the reader's attention at this initial meeting. Years and hundreds of pages elapse. Marcel, now adolescent, visits Balbec with his grandmother, and here, in the course of a stroll, meets this amazing individual face to face. . . .

> As I was coming by myself past the Casino on my way back to the hotel, I had the sensation of being watched by somebody who was not far off. I turned my head and saw a man of about forty, very tall and rather stout, with a very dark moustache, who, nervously slapping the leg of his trousers with a switch, kept fastened upon me a pair of eyes dilated with observation. Every now and then those eyes were shot through by a look of intense activity such as the sight of a person whom they do not know excites only in men to whom, for whatever reason, it suggests thoughts that would not occur to anyone else—madmen, for instance, or spies. He trained upon me a supreme stare at once bold, prudent, rapid and profound, like a last shot which one fires at an enemy at the moment when one turns to flee. . . . He gave me the impression of a " hotel crook " who had been watching my grandmother and myself for some days, and while he was planning to rob us had just discovered that I had surprised him in the act of spying ; to put me off the scent, perhaps, he was seeking only, by his new attitude,

to express boredom and detachment, but it was with an exaggeration so aggressive that his object appeared to be—at least as much as the dissipating of the suspicions that I must have had of him—to avenge a humiliation which quite unconsciously I must have inflicted on him, to give me the idea not so much that he had seen me as that I was an object of too little importance to attract his attention.[1]

Immediately after, Marcel and his grandmother meet M. de Charlus with his aunt, Mme de Villeparisis. The singular gentleman continues to affect towards the boy the same baffling mixture of condescension and contempt. They meet intermittently from now on. Marcel discovers de Charlus's family piety and outrageous pride, his art treasures and erudition. However, the enigmatic Baron still remains a personage of only secondary interest to him. Until in the opening paragraphs of *Sodome et Gomorrhe* the author suddenly tears aside the veil that had previously hidden de Charlus's true aspect from Marcel. He witnesses the meeting between Palamède and the little tailor Jupien ; overhears their conversation ; and now all is clear. The rôle of de Charlus in the novel's scheme is thenceforward psychologically clarified, and dramatically seen to be of prime importance : he is the prototype of the homosexual, the example and illustration of the author's thesis and dissertation on sexual aberration ; he is also the villain of the piece and tragically the victim of his own vice.

In the final volume, *Le Temps Retrouvé*, which opens during the 1914–1918 war, de Charlus has fallen to the lowest depths ; frequenting a homosexual brothel kept for him and some of his fellow-addicts by Jupien. And, at the end, overtaken by physical collapse and senility, he has had a stroke. The final glimpse we have of him is through the narrator's pitiful and contemptuous vision. . . .

[1] *Within a Budding Grove*, vol. ii, pp. 68–70.

I stopped the carriage . . . when I noticed a carriage
likewise about to stop. A man with glazed eyes and bent
body was deposited rather than sitting in the back of it, and
was making efforts to hold himself straight such as a child
makes when told to behave nicely. An untouched forest of
snow-white hair escaped from under his straw hat whilst a
white beard like those snow attaches to statues in public
gardens depended from his chin. . . . He seemed . . . to
have been subjected to some sort of chemical precipitation
which had the effect of making his hair shine with such a
brilliant and metallic lustre that the locks of his hair and
beard spouted like so many geysers of pure silver and clad
the aged and fallen prince with the Shakespearian majesty of
a King Lear. . . . At that very moment there passed . . .
Mme de Sainte-Euverte whom formerly the Baron did not
consider smart enough to be worth knowing. Jupien, who
was taking care of him like a child, whispered in his ear
that it was a personage he knew, Mme de Sainte-Euverte.
Immediately, with infinite trouble and with the concentration
of an invalid who wants to appear capable of movements
still painful to him, M. de Charlus uncovered, bowed, and
wished Mme de Sainte-Euverte good-day with the respect
he might have shown if she had been the Queen of France.
. . . And, more than a chorus of Sophocles on the humbled
pride of Oedipus, more even than death itself or any funeral
speech, the Baron's humble and obsequious greeting of Mme
de Sainte-Euverte proclaimed the perishable nature of earthly
grandeurs and of all human pride.[1]

Those who knew Marcel as a young man, as the darling of
the salons, have testified to his inimitable gift of mimicry.
His imitations of his intimate friends, such as Madeleine
Lemaire and Robert de Montesquiou, kept their mutual
acquaintances in fits of hysterical laughter. These perform-
ances were known as his " singeries "—monkey-business. He

[1] *Time Regained*, pp. 200–2.

also used this gift effectively in writing ; his " Pastiches " and social gossip in *Le Figaro*, though of scant literary value, nevertheless witness to his needle-sharp observation and Gallic malice. These qualities are also abundantly evident in *A La Recherche du Temps Perdu*, and never more so than in his relationship, as author, with his characters. Towards all of them, even towards his beloved grandmother, the narrator reveals a consistent and peculiar mercilessness, sometimes amounting almost to sadism. In his determination to present them scientifically, accurately, down to the last detail, and without favour, he never spares them, as the passage I have just quoted appears to prove. This applies particularly to the entire Guermantes set. He etches in the Duchesse's silliness, the Duc's boorishness, de Charlus's villainies, Robert de Saint-Loup's weaknesses, with positively Swiftian sarcasm. This seems to me another refutation of the accusation that he was a snob. Aristocracy as such undoubtedly had for Proust the gilt and glamour of tradition and history ; but none the less, for the individual aristocrat's faults of character he had no mercy at all.

Swann comes out of it, on the whole, better than the rest. Every line reveals the author's admiration for his social success, his culture, his erudition, his elegance. Yet he can hardly wait to belabour Swann with all the cruelties and indignities Odette has in store for him. He spares him not one dreg either of the tortures or of the ignominies of jealousy. Swann is aware that the entire Verdurin clan know him to be cuckolded by Odette, and yet he cannot tear himself away. Finally, when he is not even in love with her any more, he marries her. And in their salon, some years later, Odette tells her friends : " Don't take any notice of him ; he's a senile old fool." Swann does not even die " on-stage," he just fades out of the story, and not until years later, at a party, quite casually, do we learn of his death.

When first we meet Robert de Saint-Loup, we can hardly be blamed if we fall into the trap of believing that here, at last, is the hero. Marcel revels in describing the goodness and charm of this handsome, blond young demi-god, which are later recalled in his touching obituary, after he has been killed in action. We suffer with Robert under the taunts and insults of his vulgar mistress, Rachel. We appreciate with Marcel his thoughtfulness and kindness, his modesty and admiration for his friend's intellectual superiority. But no sooner have we fallen in love with this sweet-natured and chivalrous paragon, than Proust pulls us roughly out of our dream by revealing to us the vicious and sordid side of this character also.

The other nearly wholly lovable character is Françoise. Here again, however, he does not spare us the disenchantments of a full-length portrait, with her vices as well as her virtues clearly drawn ; as in the description of how she tortured the poor kitchen-maid, the " Charity of Giotto," by making her peel asparagus. Their smell made the girl feel sick, as she was pregnant, but she was about to become an unmarried mother, and this was Françoise's method of punishing her for her sin. Or he gives us a revolting description of Françoise, belabouring a wretched cockerel she was wanting to kill for dinner, but that refused to strangle easily, whilst she scolds it with rough imprecations for its refusal to die quietly.

But if, in his relations with his other characters, Proust reveals a subconscious or frequently a conscious sadism, his integrity and honesty as man and writer compel him to use the rods of flagellation equally severely on himself. His masochism seeks and finds its match in Albertine.

Albertine is the great enigma of the Proustian portrait gallery, an enigma not only to her lover who never, despite his most frantic efforts, succeeds in penetrating her mysteries,

but also an enigma to the reader. True, in her case, as in all
the others, we are given a biographical background, though
an obscure one. We are told that she is a nobody and an
orphan, without any fortune, dragged up reluctantly by an
aunt, Mme Bontemps, whose one aim and ambition is to get
the girl off her hands. We are even allowed to listen to
Albertine's own gentle lamentations over her equivocal situation. We are given her physical portrait, and it must surely
be one of the strangest in all fiction. For here is a heroine
whose eyes change colour half-way through a novel ! When
we first meet Albertine, in *A l'Ombre des Jeunes Filles en Fleurs*
she has dark eyes and dark hair, which is at first hidden by
her little " polo " cap, which later we see coiled over her
ears in thick " buns," and which, when she sleeps, spills over
the pillow. But in *La Prisonnière*, when she has come to live
in Marcel's apartment, " she had also changed physically.
Her long *blue* eyes—more narrow—had changed their shape ;
the colour was still the same, but they seemed to have become
liquefied. So much so, that when she closed them, it was
like drawn blinds, which prevent one from seeing the sea."
This odd transformation of the colour of Albertine's eyes,
which appear to have suffered a sea-change, could be partly
attributed to the fact that Marcel's first impression of her was
permanently fixed against a maritime background, but is
more probably due to the amorphousness of both her physical
appearance and her personality.

A sidelight is thrown on Albertine's lack of precise delinea-
tion in Proust's mind by what might only be a curious misprint, but which I suspect rather to be a psychological " slip,"
akin to two snapshots taken on one exposed film by an
amateur photographer. In the second volume of *Sodome et
Gomorrhe* Marcel is describing his return to Balbec and the
sharp realisation of his grandmother's death that overwhelms
him there. However, after having abandoned himself to this

sense of loss, he begins to recover, and to long once again
for Albertine and her caresses. He is sitting in the little train,
and his mind is tortured by the conflict between the claims
of the past and the temptations of the present. " So vivid a
memory had, like the stroke of a magic wand, restored the
mood that I had been gradually outgrowing for some time
past ; what had I to do with Rosemonde when my lips were
wholly possessed by the desperate longing to kiss a dead
woman." Rosemonde ? Who was she and why does she
suddenly reappear here ? Rosemonde was one of the group
of blossoming girls he had met on his first visit to Balbec.
Of the four mentioned, Rosemonde was one of the least
important. It is clear that her name has crept in at this point
in lieu of Albertine's, although the misprint has been perpetu-
ated in Mr. Scott-Moncrieff's translation of the original. It
is equally clear that it was Albertine's and not Rosemonde's
kisses he was anticipating at this point of his story. But to
confuse her with her friend is as startlingly absurd as if Shake-
speare had suddenly confused Rosalind with Olivia. The
confusion seems to me to be another indication, small but
significant, that Albertine was for Marcel not one particular
supremely important person, but one of the girls who jointly
composed the portrait of youthfulness and vitality which so
deeply attracted him, but who, separately and severally, had
a far less potent significance. Certainly to substitute for the
name of his heroine, the hero's great love, the name of one
of her girl-friends, is another author's " slip " as extraordinary
as the changing-over of the colour of her eyes.

We hear her singing in her bath, and listen as she plays
the pianola. We see Marcel and Albertine lying down side
by side on his bed, and when Françoise, coming in with the
lamp, surprises them, we wince at the sullen violence of her
enmity towards the girl. We know, definitely, that Albertine
was not Marcel's mistress in the accepted sense ; their caresses

never led to sexual consummation. At one moment she tells him how relieved she is that he does not mention that they are living together, to anyone, because they are not, in fact, lovers ; on another occasion, that she has no hopes of marriage with him, because she knows she is too poor for such a good match. By the time she comes to stay in his home, Marcel, so he tells us, no longer loves her, is bored with her, and is only compelled to keep her his prisoner because of his morbid jealousy. We overhear, ultimately with a weariness and irritability second only to their own, Marcel's and Albertine's endless discussions and arguments, their cat-and-mouse scenes ; he forever trying to entrap her, she, feinting, parrying, prevaricating, almost monotonously lying. We can't help feeling sorry for the poor little prisoner, who, with the humble patience of a penniless dependant, submits to Marcel's constant caprices and to Françoise's hatred, suspicion, and jealousy, even although it is possible she may be doing so from the mercenary motive of one day making a match with her rich young jailer. And then, one fine morning when, presumably, she has come to the end of her patience, and can no longer endure the fret, wear, tear, endless nagging and petty dramatics of their joint existence, she disappears, leaving him a short note of farewell (which, unfortunately, he does not allow us to read).

And yet, and yet . . . in spite of so many copious details, in spite of four entire volumes dedicated to her, and many sections of others, in the full-length portrait of Albertine, waking or sleeping, alive or dead, there seems to be something permanently lacking—the spark of vitality that is never missing from the other characters, however superficially sketched in they may be. This could be attributed to the fact that in writing of her, Marcel is emotionally involved as with no other one of them, not even Gilberte or the Duchesse, his two previous grand passions, and that we see her so exclusively through his eyes, and never objectively, but always through a grey veil of boredom or a red haze of jealousy, so that we can form no detached picture of her ourselves. Or, again, it may be because of the tremendous technical skill with which he shares his suspicions with the reader, hints at her secret life, without ever giving us any more definite knowledge of it than he has himself, without ever allowing us to follow her, when she leaves him, except in his company, in his imagination. We know no more where she goes, then, what she does, with whom she spends her time and takes her pleasure, than he does. All this contributes to our confusion, as much as to his. Nevertheless, whatever extraneous reasons one may seek to explain the lifelessness, the puppetry, of Albertine, one cannot, finally, avoid the suspicion that she may be no more than a mere fiction, the one entirely fictitious and synthetic character in the whole work ; that, in fact, there was no such person.

Speculation and guess-work have long supported this theory. The legend is by now pretty well established that she was, in fact, a boy, or a young man, with whom the narrator may have had an emotional relationship. If she was indeed a girl, it does seem strange that " Maman," even in her unusually lenient tolerance of her son's caprices, with her expressed fear and intense dislike of their proposed marriage, should have permitted Albertine to reside for weeks and months in the family apartment, during her own absence at Combray. And even had she been willing to accept so equivocal a situation, it seems hardly credible that " Papa " would have done the same. And the fact that " Papa " seems to have been living there at least part of the time with them (although at one point he had gone on a professional journey) is indicated, though not stressed, in the following passage :

It often happened that Albertine, either through fatigue, or the particular way of looking of an attentive person, considered thus, in a kind of meditation, it might be my father, it might be Françoise. . . .

To me, on the assumption that Albertine was a girl, the situation only becomes convincing if one imagines the three of them—Marcel, Albertine, and Françoise—sharing a flat of their own, apart from his family.

But neither was Albertine a young man, any particular young man. There were many " Alberts." One point is of great interest in connection with Albertine's sudden death, through a riding accident. Marcel Proust adored Normandy, and Balbec is a composite portrait of the seaside resorts, Cabourg and Trouville, where he stayed regularly. When his hay fever made it impossible for him to visit the flowering apple-orchards and the ancient churches on foot, he used to hire a taxi, and, with the windows carefully closed, he would have himself driven all over the country. In the first essay of the second part of *Pastiches et Mélanges* (Gallimard, 1919), entitled " En Memoire des Églises Assassinées," sub-title " Journées en Automobile," Proust describes one of these drives. The following extract from this, incidentally, enchanting essay, may be of interest here :

Engine trouble held us up until nightfall at Lisieux ; before leaving I wanted to look again at certain decorations on the façade of the cathedral, mentioned by Ruskin, but the feeble street-lighting of the town ceased altogether in the square, where Notre-Dame was almost completely plunged in obscurity. Still, I went on, wanting at least to touch with my hand the famous hedge of stone in which the porch is planted, in between whose nobly carved ranks may have passed the wedding procession of Henry II of England and Eleanor of Guyenne. But as I felt my way towards it, suddenly it was drowned in a flood of light ; the pillars emerged from the night, trunk by trunk, their stone foliage displayed vividly, in full brightness, against the shadowy background. For my ingenious chauffeur, Agostinelli, was directing his headlights on to one part of the porch after another, as I wanted to look at them, sending the ancient sculptures a salutation from the present, the light of which served only for the better reading of the lessons of the past.

And here comes the following footnote :

When I wrote the above lines I did not foresee that seven or eight years later this young man would ask to be allowed to type one of my books, would learn to fly, under the name of Marcel Swann, in which his friendship chose to combine my Christian name with the name of one of my characters, and that, at the age of twenty-six, he would be killed in an aeroplane crash, near Antibes.

Now Agostinelli and his beloved, Anna, who passed as his wife, lived for a time in Proust's household, along with Céleste Albaret (Françoise) and her husband, Odilon Albaret, who acted as Proust's chauffeur, whilst Agostinelli was secretary. There was considerable friction between the rival retainers. Moreover, Anna and Proust were mutually antagonistic. We know that none of the Proustian characters are portraits of any single one of his contemporaries, though they are composites, founded on well-known and recognisable individuals. Agostinelli had in common with Albertine an emotional attachment to the author and narrator. But he was a lover of women, particularly of Anna, who was " all the world " to him. In this connection, I think, he may well have served also as a model for the violinist Morel, beloved of the Baron de Charlus. Morel, also, was of plebeian background—his father had been valet to Marcel's uncle. Morel confesses to Marcel that his great desire would be to seduce a virgin, and under the promise of marriage, he becomes the lover of the charming young seamstress (the only Dickensian type of heroine in all Proust), the daughter of the tailor Jupien. It seems to me not improbable that Agostinelli and his relationship to Proust, especially on the financial and social side, may have served also as a model for Morel and his relationship to the Baron de Charlus.

CHAPTER IV

"THE STYLE IS THE MAN"

WHEN, after a lapse of time, one returns to Proust, there is a peculiar sense of homecoming, or, of going back to one's favourite holiday resort after years of exile. One notices with a pang of pleasure each familiar landmark : the hawthorns outside Tansonville, the water-lilies on the Vivonne ; the delicious smell of Françoise's cooking, as soon as one enters the vestibule of Aunt Léonie's house ; or the fragrance of the expensive China tea Odette de Crécy's manservant brings into her drawing-room, where she is entertaining Swann, and where it blends discreetly with her expensive scent, and with the dry, autumnal aroma of the enormous shaggy chrysanthemums in their vases and epergnes. Or one is again in the Champs-Élysées in spring, where the chestnuts are just bursting into green-golden brightness, with little Gilberte and Marcel—whose ambiguous play and conversation resemble those of two miniature grown-ups—utterly unlike simple, romping English children. One is again in the little train, puffing its way along the Normandy coast, going to visit Robert de Saint-Loup in his snug bachelor quarters in the barracks at Doncières, where enormous log fires roar up the chimney in winter, and even Marcel does not feel the draughts. If it is summer, one enjoys in anticipation the delicious food and wines of the restaurant at Rivebelle, where lovely women in silk and muslin frocks make blobs and splashes of rose-pink or azure blue in the golden light of a Renoir scene, and where, with Marcel, one gets drunk as much aesthetically as alcoholically. Happy moment ! . . .

But then the kaleidoscope changes again, and one is waiting with Marcel for his grandmother, who, at the onset of her illness has had to visit the chalet in the Champs-Élysées, and emerges, tragically untidy and upset, after the Rabelaisian female attendant has been expounding to us her philosophy of life. . . . One is listening to music with the Verdurins, to the little phrase of the sonata of Vinteuil, or one sees, from Mme Verdurin's box, the first splendid sunrise of the early Diaghilev ballets with their Bakst *décors*, whilst the magical feather-music of Stravinsky's " Firebird " caresses one's ears. . . . A Guermantes party—another, so many Guermantes parties—with Marcel one wearies of the social round.   Nevertheless, with the exquisite relief of gratified nostalgia, one knows that everything is as it was.   However far one has journeyed, however much oneself has changed, here nothing has changed ; everything remains static, permanent, constant, a slice of Time eternalised, seen, not as through a glass, darkly, but by the light of the author's genius, brightly.

How is this perfect illusion achieved ?   Although it may seem like pure magic, on investigation it turns out to be more like the conjuring trick of a master magician.   When one watches the lady being sawn in half and lets oneself be in-veigled into open-mouthed amazement, one knows, neverthe-less, that there is an explanation of the illusion, that it depends merely on expert technique, timing, and rehearsing.   So in the case of the Proustian illusion it is perfectly possible to take apart, analyse, and follow the trick intellectually without losing any of the original amazement and delight with which one has watched the performance.   On the contrary, the more one realises " how it is done," the greater becomes the enjoy-ment of the doing of it, since intellectual participation enhances the aesthetic experience.

Basically, this sense of familiarity, this intimate partaking in his scene, this feeling, of not being outside it, either in

Time or in imagination, but of being part of it, " living "
it, must be communicated to the reader by any novelist
aspiring to be considered among the great ones. Turgeniev
and Tolstoy, de Maupassant, Flaubert and Proust, Fielding,
Jane Austen, Dickens and Thackeray, Maugham and Wells,
all the great novelists have had in common this quality of
enticing the reader into their world, and making him free
of it. The fact that Proust did so is no evidence of his
uniqueness. It is merely a vindication of his right to take
his place among his peers.

But while many of the other great novelists have presented
their world impressionistically, suggesting a complete scene
or portraying an event with a few pen-strokes, in Proust's
case the picture is built up, tiny detail by tiny detail, similar
to the *pointilliste* method in painting, of which the master,
Seurat, was also an almost unique exponent. In his great
picture, " The Bathers," Seurat's brush deals as objectively
and impartially with the slightest shimmer of light on
water as with the shimmer of expression on human faces,
and so Proust, too, gives as much attention to the preparation of the asparagus for dinner by Françoise as to
the Duchesse de Guermantes' toilette when preparing for a
grand party.

The building-up of each scene begins always at the very
beginning. The season is clearly indicated, whether spring,
summer, autumn, or winter ; the weather is described, the
time of day or night, very often the precise hour, is detailed.
The quality of the light, or of the darkness, is stressed, whether
it be pearly dawn, misty evening, midday in brilliant sunshine,
or pitch-dark midnight. The dark is especially important,
because as a child, and even until much later in his life, Marcel
was subject to night-terrors and claustrophobia. His insomnia
was partly due to this claustrophobia, and some of his
most harrowing pages are those in which he describes the

agony of his first night in the strange hotel bedroom at Balbec :

> I was half dead with exhaustion, I was burning with fever ;
> I would gladly have gone to bed, but I had no night-things.
> I should have liked at least to lie down for a little while on
> the bed, but what good would that have done me, seeing that
> I should not have been able to find any rest there for that
> mass of sensations which is for each of us his sentient if not
> his material body, and that the unfamiliar objects which
> encircled that body, forcing it to set its perceptions on a
> permanent footing of a vigilant and defensive guard, would
> have kept my sight, my hearing, all my senses in a position
> as cramped and comfortless (even if I had stretched out my
> legs) as that of Cardinal La Balue in the cage in which he
> could neither stand nor sit. It is our noticing them that puts
> things in a room, our growing used to them that takes them
> away again and clears a space for us. Space there was none
> for me in my bedroom (mine in name only) at Balbec ; it
> was full of things which did not know me, which flung back
> at me the distrustful look that I had cast at them, and, without
> taking any heed of my existence, showed that I was inter-
> rupting the course of theirs. The clock . . . continued
> without a moment's interruption to utter, in an unknown
> tongue, a series of observations which must have been most
> uncomplimentary to myself, for the violet curtains listened to
> them without replying, but in an attitude such as people adopt
> who shrug their shoulders to indicate that the sight of a third
> person irritates them. . . . I was tormented by the presence
> of some little bookcases with glass fronts which ran along the
> walls, but especially by a large mirror with feet which stood
> across one corner. . . . I kept raising my eyes towards the
> fantastically high ceiling of this belvedere planted upon the
> summit of the hotel, which my grandmother had chosen for
> me ; and in that region more intimate than those in which
> we see and hear, that region in which we test the quality of
> odours, almost in the very heart of my inmost self, the smell
> of flowering grasses next launched its offensive against my last

feeble line of trenches, where I stood up to it, not without tiring myself still further, with the futile incessant defence of an anxious sniffing. Having no world, no room, no body now that was not menaced by the enemies thronging round me, invaded to the very bones by fever, I was utterly alone : I longed to die.[1]

The climate and temperature of the scene having been established, the time of day or night precisely indicated, it is then filled in, furnished with its inanimate contents, the placing of which, as on a stage, must precede the entry of the characters. Yet even the room or the objects in it have life ; an almost human kind of life that can change its aspect to correspond with the mood of its occupier.

When I was once more in the hotel [he writes at a later stage in *A l'Ombre des Jeunes Filles en Fleurs*], it was Albertine's sole image that rose from my heart and began to shine. My room seemed to me to have become suddenly a new place. Of course, for a long time past, it had not been the hostile room of my first night in it. All our lives, we go on patiently modifying the surroundings in which we dwell ; and gradually, as habit dispenses us from feeling them, we suppress the noxious elements of colour, shape and smell which were at the root of our discomfort. Nor was it any longer the room, still potent enough over my sensibility, not certainly to make me suffer, but to give me joy . . . ; not the room, wholly aesthetic, of the pictorial evening hours ; it was the room in which I had been now for so many days that I no longer saw it. And now I was just beginning again to open my eyes to it, but this time from the selfish angle which is that of love. I liked to feel that the fine big mirror across one corner, the handsome bookcases with their fronts of glass, would give Albertine, if she came to see me, a good impression of myself. Instead of a place of transit in which I would stay for a few minutes before escaping to the beach or to Rivebelle, my

[1] *Within a Budding Grove*, vol. i, pp. 342–3.

room became real and dear to me, fashioned itself anew, for I looked at and appreciated each article of its furniture with the eyes of Albertine.

The reference to the smell of flowering grasses expresses Marcel's most intense degree of suffering in the earlier, inimical, room, owing to the hay fever which tortured his respiratory organs. Throughout the novel, flowers, which he simultaneously loved and dreaded, adored and hated, play an outstanding and characteristic part in every *décor*. They, too, take on a human symbolism. When he has at last succeeded in making friends with the " flowering girls " he goes for a walk with one of them, Andrée.

Suddenly, in the little sunken path, I stopped short, touched to the heart by an exquisite memory of my childhood. I had just recognised, by the fretted and glossy leaves which it thrust out towards me, a hawthorn-bush, flowerless, alas, now that spring was over. . . . I stood still for a moment, and Andrée, with a charming divination of what was in my mind, left me to converse with the leaves of the bush. I asked them for news of the flowers, those hawthorn flowers that were like merry little girls, headstrong, provocative, pious. " The young ladies have been gone from here for a long time now," the leaves told me. . . . " Yes, I know all that, they leave about the middle of June," I answered, " but I am so delighted to see the place where they stayed when they were here. They came to see me, too, at Combray, in my room ; my mother brought them when I was ill in bed. And we used to meet on Saturday evenings, too, at the Month of Mary devotions. Can they get to them from here ? " " Oh, of course ! Why, they make a special point of having our young ladies at Saint-Denis du Desert, the church near here." " Then, if I want to see them now ? " " Oh no, not before May, next year." " But I can be sure that they will be here ? " " They come regularly, every year." " Only I don't know whether it will be easy to find the place." "Oh dear, yes ! They are so gay, the young ladies, they stop laughing only to sing hymns together, so that you can't possibly miss them, you can tell by the scent from the other end of the path." [1]

The orchid appears to have had a strong sexual signifi-cance for Proust. The Cattleya orchids given by Swann to Odette become, as it were, her banner. These orchids play an important part in their erotic relationship, for, to make love becomes, in their intimate love-language, " faire Cattleya."

Again and again he goes to botany for his analogies, of which the most daring occurs in the opening passages of *Sodome et Gomorrhe*—where he preludes his description of the first meeting of the homosexuals, the Baron de Charlus and the tailor Jupien, by the account of his observation of the fertilisation of the rare plant in the Guermantes' garden by a bumble bee. The boldness and brilliance of this passage, which is too long to quote entirely here, and which, by cutting, would lose its intensity, which depends largely on its cumula-tive effect, is one of the most impressive feats of the Proustian technique.

" *Le style, c'est l'homme.*"

Proust's favourite author in his youth was Saint-Simon, the great eighteenth-century French memoirist ; and there is a distinct echo of this period in many of the Proustian " set pieces," the descriptions of the great houses and the sumptuous parties on the Guermantes side ; as well as in the philosophis-ing, moralising, and " reflections " which constantly interrupt plot and action.

Stylistically, Proust was particularly in the manner of the earlier period when he indulged in his virtuoso's mastery of the French verb, regular and irregular, in all its richness. He

[1] *Within a Budding Grove*, vol. ii, pp. 309–10.

was addicted to the use of the subjunctive, which served him
so well in the endless clauses, sub-clauses, and parentheses of
the thick paragraphs that succeed one another sometimes un-
interruptedly for page after page. The subjunctive properly
belongs to the earlier period, the more leisurely era of French
literature, the age on which Proust chose to model his style,
and its flavour cannot altogether be rendered in translation
into a language that relies for flexibility chiefly on the use of
auxiliary verbs, as English does.

The Proustian vocabulary has an amazing variety. He is
never at a loss for a word, and almost always it is the *mot
juste*. He took immense trouble to find it ; in his original
notebooks and manuscripts the pages are a mass of corrections
and rectifications. His endless re-writing of his proof-sheets
was the despair of his printers and publishers. Robert de
Montesquiou described " his handwriting . . . illegible, inter-
locked . . . scrawling across the sheets, not even like the foot-
prints of flies, but of ants."

There is an interesting example of his capacity for taking
infinite pains in a letter to Mme Caillavet, part of which I
quoted earlier in another connection.

> I go out occasionally, when chance permits, and it is
> generally to see the hawthorns, or the furbelows of the three
> apple-trees in their ball-gowns, under a grey sky. But when,
> much more rarely, I go out not among things but people,
> the ladies' frocks, whose colours are less delicious than those
> of the apple-trees, embarrass me quite as much. For when I
> have an impression I need precise words to explain it, and I
> have not those words. So I look through books on botany,
> or architecture, or fashion-papers. And naturally, what I
> want is never there. Young Premonville, whom I mentioned
> to you the other day, asked his botany teacher about these
> things. I thanked him effusively for his information—which
> was of no help whatever.

He plied his women friends with questions on feminine
dress. Here is an anecdote told by Léon-Pierre-Quint :

> " Tell me, Madame," he asked one of his old friends, who
> had been allowed to enter his room, " what do you call that
> stuff a young girl throws over her shoulders when she is in
> evening dress ? "   " Crêpe ? "   " That's a hideous word,
> and the young girl in my book is pretty."   " A veil ? "
> " Impossible."   " A stole ? "   " No ! "   " A fur ? A scarf ?
> A foulard ? "   " Think of something else," Marcel begged
> her.

Another snapshot from the same source :

> At one o'clock in the morning, Marcel asks if he may call
> on Madame de C——" Dear Madame," he says, " nothing
> would give me greater pleasure than to see again that little
> hat, with Parma violets, you wore at the time when I was in
> love with you, when the young man I was then admired you
> (as the man I am now still admires you). . . ."   " My dear
> Marcel, that was a hat I had twenty years ago ; I haven't
> got it any more."   " That can't be possible, Madame ! You
> don't want to show it to me. You do have it, but you want
> to annoy me ; you are going to make me most unhappy."
> " But, my poor Marcel, I don't keep my old hats. Come in
> my room. Here is my cupboard. Look for yourself. . . .
> In this drawer . . . you see ? . . . in this box ? . . . nothing.
> I really can't wake up my housemaid, who is fast asleep, to
> get out all my things for you."   " Madame Daudet kept all
> her hats," the incredulous author murmurs, " I've seen them."
> " A charming idea. But I'm afraid I don't have a museum."

And he showed a similar almost obsessive interest in all
details of furnishings, decorations, works of art, and the
activities of servants, who waited on more important personages, or prepared their meals.

> Downstairs, it was the masculine element that predominated
> and made this hotel, in view of the extreme and effortless

youth of the servants, a sort of Judaeo-Christian tragedy given
bodily form and perpetually in performance. And so I could
not help repeating to myself, when I saw them, not indeed
the lines of Racine that had come into my head at the
Princesse de Guermantes's while M. de Vaugoubert stood
watching young secretaries of embassy greet M. de Charlus,
but other lines of Racine, taken this time not from *Esther*
but from *Athalie* : for in the doorway of the hall, what in
the seventeenth century was called the portico, " a flourishing
race " of young pages clustered, especially at tea-time, like
the young Israelites of Racine's choruses. But I do not
believe that one of them could have given even the vague
answer that Joas finds to satisfy Athalie when she inquires of
the infant Prince : " What is your office, then ? " for they
had none. At the most, if one had asked any of them, like
the new Queen : " But all this race, what do they then,
imprisoned in this place ? " he might have said : " I watch
the solemn pomp and bear my part." Now and then one
of the young supers would approach some more important
personage, then this young beauty would rejoin the chorus,
and, unless it were the moment for a spell of contemplative
relaxation, they would proceed with their useless, reverent,
decorative, daily evolutions. For, except on their " day off,"
" reared in seclusion from the world " and never crossing
the threshold, they led the same ecclesiastical existence as the
Levites in *Athalie*, and as I gazed at that " young and faithful
troop " playing at the foot of the steps draped with sumptuous
carpets, I felt inclined to ask myself whether I were entering
the Grand Hotel at Balbec or the Temple of Solomon.[1]

In his final volume, *Le Temps Retrouvé*, Proust gives his
theory of literary composition. He writes : " I knew very
well that my brain was a rich mineral basin, containing immense and highly varied precious deposits." This applies as
much to his style as to his content. He is well equipped for

[1] *Cities of the Plain*, vol. i, pp. 243 *et seq.*

the exploitation of his mental wealth. His descriptions of
things, of nature, of places, and of people, cover a huge range,
but they never exceed his stylistic resources. He uses dialogue
comparatively seldom, but when he does so he invariably
puts into the mouths of his characters the words that give
them life—the deliberate slanginess of the Duc de Guermantes,
the superficial witticisms of the Duchesse, the hyperbole of
his friend Bloch, the pomposities of de Norpois, the hideous
puns of Dr. Cottard, the contempt for " bores " of Mme
Verdurin, or, above all, the delicious raciness of Françoise.

There is no doubt, however, where the great weakness of
his style lies. He was addicted to an incurable prolixity and
could never conquer this failing. In his search for almost
scientific accuracy, in his anxiety to convey to the reader the
exact shades of the most subtle meanings, by analogy or
metaphor most frequently, he was led into every highway and
byway of his imagination, in search of the precise image or
symbol he required. He never returned empty-handed, and
some of his analogies are superb.

> There is edited every day in Paris, Balzac would tell us, a
> sort of spoken newspaper, more terrible than its printed
> rivals.[1]

Nevertheless, however ardently the reader desires to follow
him at his own crawling gait, through all the tortuous laby-
rinths of sentence and paragraph in endless succession which
build up his enormous picture with the inevitable drip of
water creating stalactites, one still finds it almost impossible
not to " skip," the first time, if one is primarily interested in
the story and in the fate of the characters involved in it. Only
when that curiosity has been satisfied, can one surrender as
completely as is necessary in order to enjoy Proust at leisure,
in all his magnitude and longitude.

[1] *The Captive*, p. 297.

He was not unaware of his own weaknesses. He was
conscious of his uncontrollable long-windedness.

> Indeed we may mention (interrupting for a few moments
> our narrative, which shall be resumed immediately after the
> closure of this parenthesis which opens at the moment when
> M. de Charlus, Brichot, and myself are arriving at Mme
> Verdurin's front door) we may mention . . .[1]

He knew that his method was new and his subject in certain
respects—especially *Sodome et Gomorrhe*—shocking. He had
great difficulty in finding a publisher for *Du Côté de chez
Swann*. In rejecting the manuscript, one publisher wrote to
a friend of his :

> My mind is possibly completely blocked, but I simply
> cannot understand why a gentleman should take thirty pages
> to describe how he turned round and round in his bed before
> he could get to sleep.

Originally, he thought he could tell his story in two volumes,
and in referring to the first of these he wrote :

> . . . I do not know if I told you that this book was a novel.
> At least, it is more like a novel than anything else. There
> is a gentleman who tells the story and says : " I " ; there
> are a lot of characters ; they are " planted " in this first
> volume, which means that in the second one they will do
> exactly the opposite from what one might have expected on
> reading the first. Unfortunately, from the publisher's point
> of view, this first volume contains much less narrative than
> the second. And, as regards the composition, it is so com-
> plicated that the scheme does not appear until very late, when
> all the " themes " have begun to combine with one another.
> You will realise that none of this sounds very enticing. But
> on the conditions we discussed [he had proposed paying for
> the costs of publication out of his own pocket, after the

[1] *The Captive*, p. 289.

manuscript had been several times rejected on ordinary commercial terms] I do not think M. Grasset would lose on it, and from a literary point of view I do not think the book would " lower " him.

In his dissertation at the end of *Le Temps Retrouvé* he defends himself—somewhat unconvincingly, it must be admitted—against his critics. He had shown some " sketches " for the great work to one or two of his friends.

> No one in the least understood them [he writes]. Even those who were favourably impressed . . . congratulated me on the " microscopic " thoroughness with which I had discovered them, when, on the contrary, I had used a telescope to reveal things that only appeared to be so very small, because they were at a great distance, and were, in fact, each a world. I was seeking to uncover universal laws, but I was charged, instead, with being merely in search of petty detail.

There is truth both in his own claim, and in the rebuttals of his critics. His style and method were unique, new, and at a first approach far from easy to assimilate.

In spite of certain highly dramatic moments—Swann's last visit to the Guermantes, Albertine's sudden disappearance, the meeting of de Charlus and Jupien, the fury of Madame Verdurin, when at her party for Morel the aristocracy ignore her as if she were a servant—there is throughout the work a lack of discrimination between the important and the unimportant, the relevant and the irrelevant, which gives his style an evitable monotony and drabness, a static quality.

Yet if one extracts them from the surrounding shell of verbosity, one finds, constantly, short, flashing phrases ; jewelled aphorisms, paradoxes, poetry, wit, and profundity. " As for happiness, it has only one use : to make unhappiness possible." " The true paradises are the paradises one has lost." " Like a decadent old dowager, the Faubourg Saint-

Germain only had a timid smile for the insolent servants who invaded its salons, drank its orangeade, and introduced their mistresses to it." "But it is difficult for us to believe in vice ; just as we can never believe in the genius of someone with whom only the previous evening we went to the opera." "But political passions are like all the rest, they do not last." There are gems in plenty, even if all of them have not been mined from the author's own claim ; even if some of them have a slightly hoary, historical patina, even if, occasionally, one or the other of them turns out to be paste, not precious stone. In their entirety they constitute, nevertheless, a pretty solid treasure.

The work is given its inner cohesion by the fact that it is only half-fictional, and that the other half is autobiography. It is written throughout in the first person singular, with intense subjectivity. For this reason it has an extraordinary intimacy of appeal, a quality in common with the huge number of his immensely long letters to his friends. At each stage the reader can compare the writer's emotional reactions to his own. Whether he be describing his night-terrors as a child, the calf-loves of his adolescence, his devotion to his grandmother, his ambitions and frustrations, his weaknesses and petty meannesses (which he never shirks), or his torments of jealousy, we recognise the authentic voice, we feel "the touch of a vanished hand," the agonised embarrassments of our own lost youth, the shame of our own small vices, our own small social triumphs, and great private despair.

If the comparison does not seem too far-fetched, Proust often reminds me of the perfect broadcaster. His style frequently has the intimacy, the direct personal appeal, of the disembodied voice emerging from the microphone. Time and again he seems to be talking, from a far distance, rather than writing.

The reader who surrenders at all to the Proustian magic as

a rule surrenders completely. In spite of the prolixity and
the frequent preciousness of his style, in a very short time one
has the impression not so much of reading as of listening, to an
intimate friend who, in monotonous and yet subtly dramatic
tones is speaking, to oneself, individually. Sometimes he is
giving an amusing impression, spiced piquantly and maliciously, of the ridiculous Verdurin set or the staff of the Grand
Hotel at Balbec ; sometimes he is unburdening himself of
the nightmare from which he awoke in tears the previous
night ; or he is confiding in ourselves, and in no one else,
his suspicions of the " queerness " of de Charlus ; or the
scandal of the infidelities of Odette, or the treachery of
Albertine. One gradually comes to identify oneself with his
fears and sorrows to such an extent that when Françoise
informs him, one morning, that Albertine has left him, and
hands him her letter, one is almost afraid to open it.

CHAPTER V

ONE AND ONE MAKE ONE

A LA RECHERCHE DU TEMPS PERDU ("In Search of Lost Time ") is a work with a dual personality ; in part it is a monumental record of the social and artistic life of Paris during a period covering forty years ; in part it is one of the strangest and richest autobiographies ever written. It contains a definite though intermittently recurring theme, of a metaphysical character, man's vain battle with Time, and his struggle against its eroding and corroding effects. The leitmotif of this theme, as it would be termed in a musical work, is the author's quest for the inner meaning or message of experiences in his own past, which he has failed to apprehend, and his attempt to capture their essence, in order to be able to reconstruct his past self or selves. The last volume, *Le Temps Retrouvé* (" Time Recaptured "), gives the reader the interpretive key to the work as a whole.

The preceding brief and bare outline of the plot, and the description of some of the chief characters, may at least have served to reveal its duality. For even in this crude summary of the story, and in the classification of the characters into their appropriate groupings, we can trace distinctly the two main strands. The first and more conventional of these I will call, merely for convenience' sake, the objective or " outward " story. This concerns the characters observed by the author, the events in their lives, and their bearing on the stories of other characters, including the narrator. The whole of the Swann story, from the moment of his first meeting with Odette, is part of the " outward " story, and in fact constitutes a novel within the novel. Further, the outward-facing portion of the work includes the whole *Côté de Guermantes* with its leading and minor characters, its intrigues and sub-plots.

The subjective or " inward " story is the autobiographical story of the narrator's inner as well as outer life, from childhood to maturity : his feelings, sufferings, reflections ; his physical, mental, and spiritual experiences ; his observations and analyses of society, art, music, literature, medicine, biology, metaphysics ; the theatre, history, architecture ; his ambitions and frustrations as a potential writer, his personal relationships and intimacies, notably with his mother and grandmother, with Françoise, Gilberte, Robert de Saint-Loup, and of course, especially, with Albertine. And, beyond all this, it contains a mystical-psychological strain entirely peculiar to Proust and his method ; the pre-occupation with Time and Eternity, with past and present ; with his own memory, his own sense-perceptions, the relationship between the conscious and the subconscious layers of his mind. This particular problem reaches its climax and is solved by the discoveries described in *Le Temps Retrouvé* ; and by the subsequent triumph over Time, whereby takes place the transmutation of Time into Eternity, which he achieves once he has found the key to his own psychological mysteries : the method of using his sense-perceptions to link up his conscious memory with the hitherto hidden and secret repressed realms of his subconsciousness.

The " outward " plane appears to me—in spite of its delightfully entertaining and at times enthralling qualities— the least unique and original of the two. Taken by itself, it is a monumental achievement. Nevertheless, the *roman à clef*, the social-psychological novel, was not a Proustian invention, even although his manner of handling it was almost exactly the reverse of the classical form developed by his predecessors.

The "outward" scene, however, is essential to the "inward" monologues, and as a story is closely interwoven with the narrator's own story. For he is throughout acutely aware of the relationship between himself and his social background; the events he describes in the "outward" story and the characters that come into it, suggest nearly all of his "inward" analyses and reflections. To look at the matter from another angle, his inward necessity is ceaselessly urging him into the outward world—into the theatre, where La Berma reigns; on his travels, to Venice, and especially to Balbec; into the studio of the painter Elstir, where he is first introduced to Albertine Simonet ("with one 'n'"); and into the charmed Guermantes circle. For it is crucial to his psychology that his introspection never works in a vacuum; it requires always a setting, and a solid, material setting at that, to stimulate it to the point at which it can observe his own reactions, dissect and analyse them; the "Je" viewing the "Moi" sometimes on stage, sometimes in the wings; but a "Moi" which is invariably placed in a definite spatial setting as well as in a temporal sequence, and which is never detached nor isolated, either in space or in time.

This dual personality of *A La Recherche du Temps Perdu* is no doubt largely responsible for the slowness of its success. Most readers like or prefer a straightforward story. Even if written, as in this case, in the first person singular, as many previous classical novels were, the reader still wants to be assured, if only by implication, that he is being entertained or possibly instructed, by "pure" fiction. But in Proust's case the concession was only a half-hearted one. Whether because he was incapable of sufficient emotional and intellectual detachment from his material to present a fictional picture with sufficient technical skill to make it convincing,

or whether his desire to do so was overridden by the
compulsion of his egoism, the fact remains that it is constantly
impossible, when reading a given description or analysis of
an experience, to know where to draw the line. Did this
happen to the narrator or to the author, to Marcel Proust in
person, in real life, or to the " Je," the " I " of the novel ?

On one occasion he almost takes the reader into his
confidence ; he steps out of the framework of the novel, to
which even with all his digressions he does on the whole
conform, to indulge in a rather tiresomely facetious apostrophe
to us. It is worth quoting here for the revelatory passage I
have italicised. (He is trying to remember, at a party, the
name of a certain lady, Mme d'Arpajon, which has
momentarily eluded him.)

> In that great game of hide and seek which is played in our
> memory when we seek to recapture a name, there is not any
> series of gradual approximations. We see nothing, then
> suddenly the name appears in its exact form and very different
> from what we thought we could make out. It is not the
> name that has come to us. No, I believe that, as we go on
> living, we pass our time in keeping away from the zone in
> which a name is distinct, and it was by an exercise of my
> will and attention which increased the acuteness of my inward
> vision that all of a sudden I had pierced the semi-darkness
> and seen daylight. In any case, if there are transitions between
> oblivion and memory, then, these transitions are unconscious.
> For the intermediate names through which we pass, before
> finding the real name, are themselves false, and bring us
> nowhere nearer to it. They are not even, properly speaking,
> names at all, but often mere consonants which are not to be
> found in the recaptured name. And yet, this operation of
> mind passing from a blank to reality is so mysterious, that it
> is possible after all that these false consonants are really
> handles, awkwardly held out to enable us to seize hold of
> the correct name. " *All this*," *the reader will remark*, " *tells us*

nothing as to the lady's failure to oblige ; but since you have made so long a digression, allow me, gentle author, to waste another moment of your time in telling you that it is a pity that, young as you were (or as your hero was, if he be not yourself), you had already so feeble a memory that you could not recall the name of a lady whom you knew quite well." [1]

This is almost a confession that he was being as auto-biographical as he dared. On the occasions when he did not dare, he deliberately provided himself with an alibi.

When the various volumes were in course of appearing these alibis foxed many of Proust's contemporaries. Léon Pierre-Quint began to write his admirable commentary on Proust before the final volumes had appeared. After the posthumous publication of the later ones, Pierre-Quint rewrote his own book, adding a further interpretation of their meaning. During Proust's later years a legend had begun to grow around him, based on his peculiar, hermit-like existence, alternating with rarer and rarer sorties into the world from his self-imposed isolation. Contemporaries who saw this extraordinary phenomenon, this corpse-like apparition from the sick-room suddenly appear in their midst, either in a salon at 2 a.m. or in the porter's lodge at the Ritz Hotel, naturally found a ready-made mystery man available for the building-up of the legend of this human enigma.

At that time, in the second decade of this century, the chief clue to the Proustian mystery was known only to few, and was rarely mentioned outside a closed circle. Even after his death, it was a long time until the relevant facts of his life were made public. But these facts were largely responsible for the confusion caused in his readers by his narrative ; a confusion almost wholly due to the dilemma which confronted Proust throughout his lifetime. For much as he wished to tell all, he was obliged at the same time to conceal all.

[1] *Cities of the Plain*, vol. i, pp. 71–2.

In 1895 Oscar Wilde had been sentenced to two years imprisonment with hard labour for homosexual offences. Towards the end of the nineteenth century and in the early years of the twentieth, homosexuality was rejected with the deepest abhorrence by the majority of decent people in all classes of society. There was very little study or understanding either of its physiological or psychological origins even in scientific or medical circles. Among the general public the subject was regarded as horrible and was socially taboo. The confirmed homosexual was a social outcast. Yet in that year, Marcel Proust, the fashionable young man about town, was becoming Marcel Proust the budding author, and writing *Les Plaisirs et les Jours*, of which I have already quoted part of the dedication. He had, obviously, known for some time previously of his own sexual orientation, and was deeply oppressed by the knowledge and the necessity to conceal his clandestine passions and their gratification from all those who were not of the same kind as himself.

When he came to consider the theme for the great novel he wished to write and knew that one day he would write, he decided that the subject of Sodom and Gomorrha was integral to it. The thought frightened him but it remained with him, and in due course grew into a fixed determination. But as he considered his thematic material against the background of the risks and dangers that would be involved in dealing with it—in his period—he had to find a way of telling the story in such a manner that, whilst giving all the facts, he could do so without incurring the stigma of himself being branded as an invert. The method he found for solving this problem is the basic explanation of the confusion he aroused in his readers.

A La Recherche du Temps Perdu was not written, as most conventional novels are, in chronological order. Proust's method was, like everything else about him, unique, and peculiar to himself. During his mother's lifetime he could not set about the work, for obvious reasons. Yet he began— no one knows exactly when, but it is generally assumed that it was before her death—to fill notebooks with observations, analyses, stories, that were in due course, in a most compli- cated and unanalysable fashion, to be welded into the great and complete whole. He took care to work up gradually to that part of his story which was to disclose the innermost life of the members of that secret confraternity to which he himself belonged. All that was necessary, according to a conversation quoted by André Gide in his *Journal*, was that one should never incriminate the first person singular when writing on this subject. " *Vous pouvez tout raconter, mais à condition de ne jamais dire ' Je.' "*

The method he finally adopted had a threefold aspect. Firstly, he begins *Sodome et Gomorrhe* with a long, pseudo- scientific treatise on the fertilisation of a rare plant by an equally rare insect. He then introduces the theme of the first meeting of the Baron de Charlus and the tailor Jupien. This is described at length as the naturalist Fabre might have described the mating of two insects ; with no relevant detail left out, but also with the most scrupulous detachment on the part of the narrator and observer. Later follows a tremendously long and moving description of the secret lives, the sufferings, the loneliness, of homosexuals, in which the author plainly tries to enlist the sympathy of his uninitiated readers for the subjects of his detailed analysis. But there is never a hint that might induce even the more perspicacious reader to imagine the author to be writing about himself ; Proust to be baring the sad and guilty soul of Marcel to the world. On the contrary, when he reverts once more to the narrator's tale, he goes out of his way to emphasise his heterosexuality, so that, parallel with the story of the Baron de Charlus's passion for the young man, the violinist Morel, is placed the story of the narrator's love affair with the young girl, Albertine Simonet.

For these reasons *Sodome et Gomorrhe* reveals more clearly than any other aspect of *A La Recherche* the curious and complicated intertwinings of the objective and subjective sides of the work. Proust the author and " Je," the narrator, are one and the same person. The difference between them lies in the need of Proust the author to use the narrator as an alibi when circumstances require that the autobiographical reminiscences and admissions should not blemish the social reputation of Proust the man.

CHAPTER VI

"THE CHILD IS FATHER . . ."

AT the beginning of this brief study I said that the biographer or critic of Marcel Proust the man had to contend with one supreme rival : Marcel Proust the author. Yet this statement could be inverted, and one might equally say that never was an author so helpful, posthumously, to a student of his life and work. For Proust's novel is founded in its subjective aspect so closely on his own life, experience, and inner development, that we can follow them minutely, from childhood to maturity, through his own self-revelations.

Nevertheless, his apparent lack of reticence, in spite of the impression of complete frankness and candour it might superficially give, is largely illusory. It is, in fact, a cunningly and superbly contrived alibi to hide or obscure what he does not wish to communicate, not even to himself.

It is difficult to imagine that Proust's uncanny intuition, backed by his indefatigable power of analysis, expecially of self-analysis, was unaware of his fundamental psychological conflicts. The fact that in spite of so much that is revealed so much is still withheld may perhaps be attributed to the psychological " censorship " most human beings have to exercise over their subconsciousness in order to be able to lead everyday normal lives. Proust is the last person to have led such a life ; his health, his mind, his genius, none of them were exactly " normal." Every day and every night meant for him a fresh, sometimes agonising, effort of adaptation to living ; even, often, to such a simple physiological activity as breathing. However he solved or failed to solve this problem as a man the most moving part of his work as an author is the autobiographical " inward " revelation to which the effort to do so urged him on.

The " Search " which is the main theme of the auto-biographical content of *A La Recherche du Temps Perdu* is not an objective account of the facts of his life, but a highly subjective rationalisation of them ; a form of special pleading and his *apologia pro vita sua*. This " Search " is not alone for lost Time or Times, but even more anxiously, more passion-ately, for his lost self or selves, beginning with himself as a small child.

Having, in the first part of the first volume of *Du Côté de Chez Swann*, reconstructed his entire childhood, he is able to proceed from there, in all the subsequent volumes, to re-create himself as an adolescent, as a youth, and finally, as a mature adult. When, in the last volume, *Le Temps Retrouvé*, he has been able to complete the self-portrait to his satisfaction he is ready for Death, to whom he very soon afterwards surrendered.

Let us then take his own story, the facts as he presents them, and his interpretation of them, as the basis of our investigation and divination of what objectively may have lain behind them, hidden even from himself.

One of the fundamental causes of his psychological mal-adjustment was his emotional bias towards his parents. He adored his mother. His love for her, from his infancy until her death in 1905, was the emotional mainspring of his life. When she died he was orphaned, at the age of thirty-four ; an age at which a normal adult has long outgrown the terrifying loneliness of knowing himself to be an orphan. At the onset of full maturity Marcel's reaction to the loss of his mother was no different from what it might have been had she died during his childhood or adolescence. . He was, and

remained until the end of his days, a little boy lost. Yet
perhaps the most significant aspect of their relationship was
the fact that only after this outwardly tragic turning-point in
his life was he able to " find himself ", as a writer.

In Chapter I, page 18, I quoted a passage from the
dedication of Proust's youthful *Les Plaisirs et les Jours* in
which the budding author, at the age of twenty-five, describes
his childish emotions aroused by the Biblical story of Noah's
Ark. He identified the Ark with his sick-room and his own
feelings of claustrophobia were transferred to Noah. His
mother, who watched over him, was the dove, his messenger
to the outer world. He could not bear her to leave him and
waited anxiously for her return. Whenever his health
improved she felt it incumbent on herself to curb the maternal
tenderness and to adopt a more severe tone in order to train
the child to face up to normal life. But Madame Proust
never managed to strike a balance between the excessively
anxious, adoring watchfulness the invalid required and
demanded and the discipline to be imposed if he were to
be weaned from his morbid dependence on her maternal
love.

The first volume of *A La Recherche du Temps Perdu* appeared
in 1913, when the author was forty-two ; the last, in 1926,
posthumously. The work was completed in 1922, exactly
twenty-two years after the publication of *Les Plaisirs et les
Jours*. Yet we find that this enormous work opens and
concludes with an elaboration on the maternal theme, exactly
in the vein of the preface to *Les Plaisirs et les Jours*. If ever
there was a case in which one might legitimately claim
that " *plus ç'a change, plus c'est la même chose*,' it was surely
the relationship between Marcel Proust and his mother.
Nevertheless, a change or rather a variation on the theme
has occurred by the end of *Le Temps Retrouvé*, written after
Madame Proust's death. Marcel had come to blame his

him to conceal from her the theme which was to be the
principal emotional basis of his novel : the theme of Sodom
and Gomorrha.

Let us, however, now turn to his earlier work, *Les Plaisirs
et les Jours*.   A consideration of its style and contents will, I
think, be helpful in several directions.   Although, reading it
nowadays, in the modern edition published by Gallimard in
1925, one does not get the full flavour of its earlier form,
the contents and the style are nevertheless still of great interest.
The original edition, pretentiously and expensively published
with floral embellishments by Madeleine Lemaire and musical
contributions by Reynaldo Hahn, was not well received.
And it is indeed difficult to realise that some of the little pieces
that make up the collection of short stories and essays of
which it consists, were written by a young man of twenty-five
and not by an adolescent.   The style is a curious agglomerate
of literary pastiche in which are embedded occasional gleams
of genius ;   many passages are mere " period," dated and
tiresome ;   others contain some real Proustian gems.   In the
first story, entitled " *La Mort de Baldassare Silvande, Vicomte
de Sylvannie* "—note the pretentious title—the boy Alexis is
visiting his Uncle Baldassare, dying of a painful disease.   The
uncle is reading a letter from the Duke of Parma :

> " MY DEAR BALDASSARE,—How bored I am not to be able
> to see you, etc., etc."   As the Prince's amiability revealed
> itself, Baldassare's face softened and glowed with happy
> confidence.   But on a sudden, perhaps because he wished to
> hide a pleasure he did not think of a very high order, he
> clenched his teeth and made the pretty little vulgar grimace
> that Alexis had thought forever banished from his features,
> calmed by approaching death.   This little grimace, which
> made Baldassare's lips crease as in the past, opened Alexis's
> eyes ;   for whilst he was with his uncle he had thought, had
> wanted, to study the face of a dying man who was being

freed forever from vulgar reality, and where he had thought
now to find only a heroically restrained, sadly tender, heavenly
and disillusioned smile.   And now he did not doubt that . . .
in the invalid's gaiety, his desire to visit the theatre, there was
neither dissimulation nor courage, but that, having come so
close to dying, Baldassare was still thinking of nothing but
living.

The theme of death runs through the short stories in this
small collection, just as, years later, it will run through *A La
Recherche du Temps Perdu*.   And the same is true of two other
of the main Proustian themes ; the sense of guilt in connection
with sexual passion, and the supreme emotion he identified
with sexual love, the emotion of jealousy.

The guilt-theme is to the fore in " The Confessions of a
Young Girl "—a rather unpleasant young girl, who recalls
both the author in relation to his mother, and Albertine.
For the heroine of this little tale, which has a disagreeably
moralising tone all the way through, is not much more
typically a " young girl " than Albertine is.   She recalls
much more the young man that Marcel probably then was.
She tells how she strove to live up to her mother's wishes
for her, to be good and industrious, happily married and
virtuous ; how she " fell by the wayside " and indulged in
dubious sexual play with her young men friends ; as the
young would nowadays call it, in " petting-parties " ; and
how, on one such occasion, her mother, whom she adored,
strolling on the balcony, glanced through the window and
discovered her doing so, when, overcome by the shock, she
fell from the balcony and was killed.   Whereupon the
daughter had attempted to shoot herself and having failed to
die instantly, makes this confession whilst waiting for death.
As a story it is rather silly ; but as autobiography it is curiously
interesting.

The best story in the collection and most closely fore-

patient's agonising symptoms as unimportant and " merely "
nervous ; the patient resented the doctor's indifference and
still more his brother's casual dismissal of his complaints of
sleeplessness. It is to be borne in mind that Marcel's younger
brother Robert was a medical student, a hale and hearty
youthful edition of Dr. Proust. It is also worth noting that
this is the only reference to a fictional brother in the story of
Honoré and Françoise, and the reference appears to be a
cri du cœur or perhaps the working-off of a grudge by the
young author, carried away, in describing the symptoms, not
of the dying Honoré but of the living Marcel, into a flight
of autobiography pure and simple. This blending of fiction
and autobiography is intrinsic to his manner of writing, as
will be proved conclusively in *A La Recherche du Temps Perdu*.

If Proust's love for his mother was admittedly quite
unusually obsessive, there is little evidence of any comparable
emotion towards his father. As he presents their relationship
in his novel, he appears to have felt respect, the typically
French filial piety, but little tenderness for him. He never
places his father directly in an unfavourable light, but neither
does he portray him as a person to be loved. There is little
evidence of affection towards him, and none of intimacy.
The father causes the son considerable uneasiness of conscience,
chiefly in regard to the youth's " idleness " and his disinclina-
tion to take up a career. He describes in detail how his father
wishes him to go into the diplomatic service, and with this
end in view, introduces him to several of his influential
friends, especially the stupid and pompous ex-Ambassador,
M. de Norpois. Marcel is disgusted by de Norpois's contempt
for men of letters, for, already, he knows himself to be a
writer by vocation. M. de Norpois, when asked his opinion
on members of the literary profession by the young man's
father, disdainfully dismisses them as " flute-players," mere
entertainers. Marcel, whose contempt for the ex-Ambassador's

ignorance of letters and lack of culture is even more profound,
feels that if de Norpois is a typical diplomat, then he himself
would prefer to be a "mere flute-player." His father is
disappointed in him by his refusal to take up a "serious"
profession, but makes no attempt to coerce him. For this the
son is grateful but suffers feelings of guilt and remorse.

The truth probably is that Dr. Proust also had feelings of
guilt and remorse towards his elder son. He, a thoroughly
healthy man, had produced this asthmatic weakling; an
eminent medical man, he was unable to cure his own child.
Dr. Proust seems, occasionally, mildly to have reproached his
wife for spoiling the boy so unreservedly; and yet, when
the child had one of his *crises de nerfs* and wept madly
because his mother had not come to put him to bed, the
father (in the novel) says to his wife: "But we are not
murderers; go and comfort him." In their home, abetted
and protected by his mother, Marcel led his own life, never
getting up until after his father had left the apartment, and
sometimes sleeping when the doctor came home. Then
Mme Proust would say to her husband: "Please don't make
a noise; it might wake him up." And the guilty father
would obey. He could never understand Marcel's passion for
"society," nor what all those grand people saw in the
boy; yet perhaps he was flattered to find that Marcel could
draw men and women of title, artists and writers, to his
unpretentious though comfortable bourgeois home, and he
never begrudged him money. Perhaps he was even secretly
gratified that his son, who would obviously never make his
mark as a professional man, at least had this social success.

Marcel undoubtedly resented, despised, and yet reluctantly
admired and envied his father. His emotions towards him
found two outlets, two forms of release. In real life, he
developed a fierce hatred and contempt for "the doctors."
As soon as he was his own master, he refused to allow any

medical man to advise him, and invented a peculiar treatment and regime of his own for his ailment. His father had been a specialist, a pioneer of great distinction, in the field of hygiene. Marcel spent his later years in a condition of squalor and an atmosphere of " fug " as far removed as possible from the most elementary hygienic practices. In *A La Recherche du Temps Perdu* one of the most vulgar characters, whose idiosyncracies, attitudes, expressions, horrible puns, the author flays mercilessly, is Dr. Cottard, the eminent physician and professor of medicine. Yet he tells with complete honesty how when he, the narrator, is gravely ill, Cottard is called in and prescribes a treatment which the patient at first violently rejects but which, when he in desperation agrees to follow it, instantly relieves him.

So for his mother he feels a passionate love, often however overshadowed by bitter criticism; for his father a cold, almost glacial, respect. These are the rationalisations of his guilt-feelings towards his parents, guilt-feelings largely due to a deep repressed resentment against them both; against the creators of his poor weak body, which is his life-long handicap, and sets him apart from his lucky, healthy, fellow-creatures.

Yet his most severe blame is reserved, with his masochistic but admirable honesty, for himself. Whilst he stubbornly cherishes his determination " to write, one day," and has unshakable confidence and belief in his literary talent, he knows it to be dammed, pent-up within him, by feelings of inferiority and guilt, by laziness and lack of will-power. Time and again he tries to write, only to be defeated by a sense of profound discouragement. The more his parents urge him on, the less he feels he can justify their hopes in him. In spite of a phenomenal memory, vast reading, wide culture, a passionate interest in his fellow-creatures, one ingredient seems to be lacking from his equipment : the catalytic element that will stimulate these faculties, that will precipitate the psychological action necessary before his creative power can break down his inhibitions and repressions.

As he describes his life it can easily appear, at first sight, to have consisted of an endless succession of futilities and frivolities. He was an admitted social climber. An amateurish though sincere passion for music, the theatre, and art ; a slightly more solid knowledge of literature, history, and architecture ; a deep, mystical love of nature ; none of these interests in themselves are particularly original or impressive. Many of the aesthetic disquisitions with which that unfortunate prolixity of his litters the work, are to-day out-moded, " dated," and have a fustian flavour. They induce drowsiness and tempt the " skipper." Critics like H. G. Wells—a typical Fabian, a lifelong student of science, economics, and sociology, a bold and genial intellectual adventurer—cannot be too harshly blamed if a superficial reading of the English trans-lation of Proust, together with a temperamental incapacity to see below the frequently frothy surface of *A La Recherche du Temps Perdu*, gave them the impression that it would be a waste of their own time to attempt to follow the author in his search. For a great deal of his time is spent on, and a great deal of space is unnecessarily occupied, by apparent trivialities.

Marcel did take the ritual of the salons, the social protocol, the pseudo-elegant occupations of the idle aristocracy with a solemnity that frequently verged on the ridiculous. He had no career, no profession ; he never worked, as that term is understood by those who identify it only with working for a living, although he was always writing, taking notes. Yet none of his critics was more acutely aware of his weaknesses than he was. In page after page of lamentation, self-reproach, he returns to the attack on himself.

Yet what a superficial and short-sighted attitude is displayed by his denigrators ! One might as well say that Fabre, the

great French naturalist and stylist, " only " wrote about insects,
whereas, in fact, there is a distinct affinity between the widow
spider and the widow Verdurin, of which the novelist may
even have been conscious. The age of Proust was perhaps
the last age of leisure Europe was to know, except for brief
intervals between the two world wars; the last age of
economic stability for the middle class, the sunset of the old
aristocratic French social and intellectual tradition, which, ever
since the days of the Roi Soleil, the Grand Siècle, the period
of Molière and Racine, had fructified all French culture, art,
and literature. Proust himself, in *Le Temps Retrouvé*, shows
how clearly he was aware that the trailing clouds of glory
were fading from rose-pink to grey. Yet whilst from one
angle he did see himself as the recorder of the social scene of
his day, from another he took his background very much for
granted, and would have done so, one feels, had he lived at
any other period, in any other circumstances, although it is
unimaginable that he could have been anything but a Parisian,
a Frenchman.

For his chief psychological pre-occupation was with himself,
with his inward vision of himself. In the last resort, it is as a
setting for himself that he builds up his whole vast panorama.

Proust returns again and again to the theme of Death; to
his fear and horror of death; to the various guises and
disguises under which death sneaks up to its victim; to the
tricks and subterfuges by which his prey seeks to elude him.

> The death of Swann had been a crushing blow to me at
> the time. The death of Swann! Swann, in this phrase, is
> something more than a noun in the possessive case. I mean
> by it his own particular death, the death allotted by destiny
> to the service of Swann. For we talk of " death " for
> convenience, but there are almost as many different deaths as
> there are people. We are not equipped with a sense that
> would enable us to see, moving at every speed in every

direction, these deaths, the active deaths aimed by destiny at
this person or that. Often there are deaths that will not be
entirely relieved of their duties until two or even three years
later. They come in haste to plant a tumour in the side of
a Swann, then depart to attend to their other duties, returning
only when, the surgeons having performed their operation,
it is necessary to plant the tumour there afresh. Then comes
the moment when we read in the *Gaulois* that Swann's health
has been causing anxiety but that he is now making an
excellent recovery. Then, a few minutes before the breath
leaves our body, death, like a sister of charity who has come
to nurse, rather than to destroy us, enters to preside over our
last moments, crowns with a supreme halo the cold and
stiffening creature whose heart has ceased to beat. And it is
this diversity among deaths, the mystery of their circuits, the
colour of their fatal badge, that makes so impressive a
paragraph in the newspapers such as this :

" We regret to learn that M. Charles Swann passed away
yesterday at his residence in Paris, after a long and painful
illness. A Parisian whose intellectual gifts were widely
appreciated, a discriminating but steadfastly loyal friend, he
will be universally regretted, in those literary and artistic
circles where the soundness and refinement of his taste made
him a willing and a welcome guest, as well as at the Jockey
Club of which he was one of the oldest and most respected
members. He belonged also to the Union and Agricole. He
had recently resigned his membership of the Rue Royale.
His personal appearance and eminently distinguished bearing
never failed to arouse public interest at all the great events
of the musical and artistic seasons, especially at private views,
at which he was a regular attendant until, during the last
years of his life, he became almost entirely confined to the
house. The funeral will take place, etc." [1]

The death of the great writer whom he calls Bergotte, whose
character and style are said to have been based on those of

---

[1] *The Captive*, pp. 267 et seq.

himself, but nevertheless, for new reasons, reiterated his
previous prohibition. Bergotte returned to one of his earlier
doctors, a man who flattered himself that he was a wit,
especially in the presence of a master of the pen, and who,
if Bergotte suggested : " It seems to me that Dr. ' X ' told
me—in the past, of course—that to do so would inflame my
kidneys and my brain "—smiled maliciously, raised his finger
and stated : " I said use ; I did not say abuse. Obviously,
every remedy, if one exaggerates its use, becomes a double-
edged weapon. . . ." By each of these doctors Bergotte
was ordered something that common sense had made him
forbid himself since many years. After a few weeks his former
symptoms returned, his later ones were aggravated. Driven
crazy by constant suffering, added to insomnia interrupted
only by short nightmares, Bergotte saw no more doctors, but
tried, both with success and with excess, various narcotics. . . .[1]

A critic had written of the " View of Delft " by the artist
Vermeer (who was Proust's favourite painter), praising the
painting of a little bit of yellow wall in this picture, and
Bergotte, in spite of his illness, decides to go and see the
picture again. This is exactly what happened in Proust's
own case. Proust left his sick-bed and his room, half-starved
and doped as he was, and asked a friend to take him to the
exhibition where this picture was on view. But the effort
proved too much for him ; he collapsed there, and had to be
taken home.

In *Le Temps Retrouvé* the conquest of Time is equated with
the triumph over Death. But before going further into his
attitude towards the problem of death, it might be illumin-
ating to consider his attitude towards life. For both attitudes
are, as one might expect, closely intertwined and connected.
In both cases there was, on his part, a permanent psychological
conflict and ambivalence. Towards death, a conscious,

[1] *The Captive*, pp. 246 (last line) to 248.

rationalised resistance which masked a repressed willingness to surrender at the least solicitation ; towards life, a sub-conscious, carefully disguised resistance, which was only broken down at almost the penultimate moment, as we shall see later, in a manner so dramatic that it constitutes the most thrilling revelation of the entire work, both to its author and to the reader.

The various forms taken by his resistance to life, to the difficulties of living, begin to appear almost from the first pages of *Du Côté de chez Swann*, in his descriptions of his sufferings and his adaptation to them, in early childhood.[1] His dependence on his mother ; his lack of will-power ; his incapacity to adapt himself to any new environment without acute physical and mental agony ; in brief, his shrinking, subconsciously and consciously, from all the activities which to a normal person constitute living.   When he was still a small child, he found for himself an almost completely secure refuge from life's exigencies in semi-invalidism and hypochondria.   Whether his asthma, hay fever, and their psychological effects produced this compensatory way of release, or whether his subconscious resistance to becoming a really healthy person, capable of leading an active life, aggravated his physical condition, is not, in this connection, decisive.   Here we are concerned primarily with the effect rather than the cause.   But as a matter of passing interest, it may be worth while to recall the portrait of such a psycho-logical type by another great novelist, by Thomas Mann, author of *Buddenbrucks* and *The Magic Mountain*, with its unforgettable analysis of the Proustian hero, whom he describes as " life's delicate child " and in whom he traces the gradual decline of a healthy body in which resides an unhealthy mind.

Marcel was certainly " life's delicate child."   In his novel

[1] Cf. pp. 18–19.

the doctor's opposition, to allow him to go to the theatre to see " La Berma " (Sarah Bernhardt) for whom he had a passionate admiration, but in whom, as is usual with him, he is at first disappointed, when he compares her actual performance with his anticipation of it. His excursions into the Guermantes' world, his regular attendance at the great social rituals of the Faubourg Saint-Germain, need no emphasis. In the opening paragraphs of *Le Temps Retrouvé* he tells us he has spent a long time in a nursing home. On emerging from it he is feeling more hopelessly pessimistic than ever about his capacity to become a successful writer—he has left it until almost too late, he recognises—so he decides to return just once more to society (since a little more wasting of his futile time will not now make much difference) in order to " distract " himself.

Until almost the very end, the " insatiable curiosity " of the man and the writer, his interest in his fellow-creatures, his love of life and yearning for company, occasionally still freed themselves from the bondage of the spartan restrictions with which his fears and phobias had so long been strangling them, and, as it were, had a night out. Léon-Pierre-Quint gives two astonishing snapshots of Proust soon after the success of *A l'Ombre des Jeunes Filles en Fleurs* had, to his intense delight, made something of a social and literary lion of him.

> Eight hundred and seventy letters of congratulation—" too kind "—arrived for him from all parts of the world. How reply to them all ? His gratitude exceeds his means of expressing it. In order to return his immense thanks he gives a series of magnificent dinners at the Ritz to those who helped him to gain, or who awarded him, the Prix Goncourt. As in the past, when he entertained at home, he invites the men of letters, the Academicians, the critics, to meet a few social leaders. Owing to his nervous attacks, he never knew from day to day whether he would be well enough to receive

his guests and, in consequence, he never invited them until the last moment. He orders a dinner for fifteen people. He awaits them, in a private dining-room, in front of an enormous table, laid ready, and lavishly decorated with scentless flowers. Finally, perhaps two guests, who happened accidentally to be free on that particular evening, turn up. He renews his invitations. The tips he gives the waiters are bigger than ever. Intoxicated by his success his unbounded generosity causes him to spend the entire prize of 5,000 francs in a few nights. . . .

When he awoke, generally in the middle of the night, and did not wish to be alone, he would send Odilon [the husband of Céleste Albaret, his housekeeper] with his taxi, to fetch one of his friends. The friend was generally either out, or was asleep. But, as one could never see Proust except at these inconvenient hours, one put up with it, got up, dressed, and allowed oneself to be driven there.

He was, of course, in bed, with a scarf around his neck. When one arrived, very often he got out of bed in all his clothes, wearing white or black cotton gloves, several pairs of socks, and his white shirt-front, all crumpled up.

" Wait a few minutes before you talk to me," he would say, in a half-dead voice. " The caffeine I've just taken, to wake me up, has not yet worked ; I can't open my mouth. But I already feel the moment approaching when I shall be better."

And as life gradually returned to him he would plunge into a long and brilliant discourse which revealed that this astounding recluse had read all the latest books, had been writing masses of long, detailed, and complicated letters, and had been following all the news of the day, financial, political, and social.

It seems probable that his fear of life was closely related, psychologically, to his fear of love. The emotion of love was to him one of almost unmitigated suffering ; he never

brilliant creatures, Albertine is the brightest and most restless ;
compared with her allure, her gaiety, her insatiable appetite
for pleasure, even Andrée, Gisèle, Rosemonde, seem occasionally staid and sedate.

It is this superabundance of life and vitality that attracts
Marcel to Albertine, as the lamp attracts the moth. They
are as complementary, as contradictory, as incapable of union
as sunlight and shadow, as day and night. And just as, in
the old legends and tales of mythology, night and day are
constantly at war, one endeavouring to defeat and capture,
hold and imprison the other, so the relationship between
these ill-matched lovers becomes one long conflict—on his
part to bind and fetter, on hers, to escape.

The fact that Albertine dies suddenly, romantically, at the
height of her youth and beauty, as Agostinelli died, is, apart
from its autobiographical implications, a stroke of literary
genius. For, at one moment, she is there, in all her youthful
exuberance. The next, she has ceased to exist. But she never
fades, never wilts away, is never worn down by advancing
age, never succumbs to illness and decay. Always she remains
young, fair, desirable, and mysterious.

> Bold Lover, never, never canst thou kiss,
> Though winning near the goal—yet do not grieve ;
> She cannot fade, though thou hast not thy bliss,
> For ever wilt thou love, and she be fair !

But he does not love forever. In fact, he has no desire
to love, but to work through and to forget. His whole
objective as far as Albertine was concerned was, in the
beginning, to conquer her, break her, tame her. She
countered his manœuvres with the resiliency of bamboo ; she
submitted temporarily, even tried to bend herself to his will.
But she could never be broken in. Ultimately, as her magnetic
vitality could not be eliminated in any other way she had to

be killed, quickly and ruthlessly. For so long as she lived
there could be no peace for him. The butterfly would
inevitably have escaped from the net ; the drab insect could
not pin her down, neatly, her fluttering wings forever stilled,
for his own appeasement. For a short time he succeeded in
capturing her but he could not hold her. Life and love,
personified by Albertine, were not for Marcel.

For a long time after her death he was still unable to resolve
the situation to his satisfaction. Yet it *had* to be resolved
before he could feel himself free once more to continue his
own half-moribund existence. With a hideous necrophilism
he still has to pursue, to hunt, to detect, posthumously, the
secrets of her love-life, even when she is no longer alive to be
spied upon, interrogated, lectured. The reason is fairly clear :
before he can win back his own peace of mind he has to
reconstitute her, recreate her, synthetically, in order to be
able to destroy her in his memory as she was destroyed by
death. Before he can resign himself to his own death-in-life
he must eliminate from his consciousness Albertine's life-in-
death. When he has succeeded in doing this, but only then,
can he find some kind of emotional release, regain his
emotional equilibrium. There is an almost horribly morbid
ignoble quality about this post-mortem detective investigation
of his into Albertine's past love-life ; his conversations with
Andrée about her, his written inquiries addressed to anyone
who might have known her, even slightly ; his burrowings
and molings. The fact that she was, or he suspected her of
having been, a Lesbian, is not important in this connection.
What mattered was the sex-life she had enjoyed with some
other lover, any other lover, or lovers, than himself ; the
ultimate satisfaction denied to him.

Incidentally, depressing as the account of this investigation
is, it reveals with the utmost sharpness the fine details of the
Proustian method ; the obstinacy and stubbornness with

subconscious, was his solution of the major problem, his incapacity to adapt to the thought of living. For the fear of life cannot be dealt with so easily ; the thought of living cannot be banished to a remote future, since every day's rising means a new birth, a confrontation with immediate and urgent problems that have to be either overcome or resolved. Turning away from this imperative, without consciously admitting his incapacity to adapt to normal life, he indulged in every possible form of escapism—chronic invalidism, hypochondria, lack of " will-power " and mental concentration, reluctance to " strengthen his will," " laziness," and the partial paralysis of his creative talent. He even went so far as to apportion part of the blame for these weaknesses of his to his mother, to her spoiling and mollycoddling of him, perhaps in some manner to avenge his grudge against her for having given birth to so sickly a child, doomed to carry the burden of ill-health throughout his life. All these were his different psychological tricks of adaptation and compensation, his techniques for refusing the responsibilities of living, and surrendering with as little mental inconvenience as possible to the attractive idea of losing, abandoning, the unsatisfactory personality he was, in death.

His second, more precisely conscious and deliberate rationalisation, was to dwell at great length, in his thoughts and writing, in pseudo-metaphysical analysis, on death, the intellectualisation of his longing to be done with the problems of living. " He realised what a terrifying thing it is to breathe, to live."

Only when he finds an incentive to live, or rather the stimulus that compels him to adapt his will and his consciousness to the problem of living, only when he at last *wants* to live, actively, in order to write, does his detailed account of his protracted struggle to ward off the ill-health that was then genuinely and rapidly overtaking him, and to postpone the victory of Death before he was ready to lay down his pen, really convince one of his sincerity. The pages in *Le Temps Retrouvé*, in which this struggle is described, carry complete conviction. For only when at last he knew himself to be able to begin to write his book, had a passionate desire to write it, after having found the key which released his until then inhibited will-power, so that he thought he would be able to carry out the tremendous task he had set himself, of creating one of the longest works of fiction ever written— only then did he really, honestly, and sincerely fear death, rebel against the thought of his physical end, before he was mentally and spiritually ready for it. And, once that had become clear to him, he did in the most extraordinary manner manage for sixteen years to ward off his death until he had accomplished his task.

But the necessity he then felt to recreate his whole past, and with it himself, was due, not to the fear of death, but to the profound compulsion within him to rewrite, because he could no longer relive, his life.

CHAPTER VII

RESURRECTION

WE have now considered *A La Recherche du Temps Perdu* as a novel and an autobiography ; as a social and a psychological portrait. There still remains for investigation, however, what to me is its most poignant, most beautiful, and most significant aspect—its spiritual content or message.

Before, however, we begin this last exploration, we must glance at certain preliminary intimations of what is to be revealed in the final volume. Mountains do not usually rise, stark, out of a flat plain. They are seen towering in the distance, a long way off. But to reach them the traveller is obliged to approach them through gradually rising foothills, to begin to climb slowly, in preparation for the last steep ascent. The very peak and summit of the Proustian experience must be approached in a similar manner, as, indeed, it was approached by Proust himself.

For his quest was throughout both the novel and his life the search for his own intrinsic reality, which normally eluded his conscious seeking. He found that only by, as it were, cheating or cajoling his alert and critical conscious mind could he come within reach of it. So he was forever on the look-out for those moments in his waking life when his intellect and will were not functioning with full activity ; for only in those moments, it seemed to him, did he come within tentative reach of the mysterious and elusive self in whose pursuit he was forever engaged.

At the very outset of the novel, he deals with this pre-

occupation. He notes that when dropping off to sleep, and
especially when awakening, certain things happen to or in
his mind which do not occur during full wakefulness.
Intimations . . . I do not think it is inapposite here to
recall the best lines known to me on those mysterious
messengers—

> Those obstinate questionings
> Of sense and outward things
> Fallings from us, vanishings ;
> Blank misgivings of a Creature
> Moving about in worlds not realized,
> High instincts before which our mortal Nature
> Did tremble like a guilty thing surprised. . . .
> Those shadowy recollections,
> Which, be they what they may,
> Are yet the fountain-light of all our day,
> Are yet a master-light of all our seeing ;
> Uphold us, cherish, and have power to make
> Our noisy years seem moments in the being
> Of the eternal Silence : truths that wake,
> To perish never. . . .

As we know, Marcel Proust was not a practising Christian,
nor was he a Jew. His agnosticism was of his period ; like
most intellectuals of his time he paid tribute to the discoveries
of contemporaneous biology, based on Darwinism and its
implications regarding the origins of man. Nevertheless, his
mysticism was profound and genuine. It is curious that
among all the millions of words he wrote, there is only one
passage that expresses it overtly and even then in terms of great
caution. This passage—at the end of the superb narration of
the death of the writer Bergotte, which, as we know, was
in some of its most poignant details autobiographical—bears
a curious and moving resemblance to Wordsworth's lines on

" Intimations of Immortality in Early Childhood " which I
have just quoted.

> ". . . He was dead. Permanently dead ? Who shall say ?
> Certainly our experiments in spiritualism prove no more
> than the dogmas of religion that the soul survives death. All
> that we can say is that everything is *arranged in this life as though
> we entered it carrying the burden of obligations contracted in a
> former life* ; there is no reason inherent in the conditions of
> life on this earth that can make us consider ourselves obliged
> to do good. . . . All these obligations which have not their
> sanction in our present life seem to belong to a different world,
> founded upon kindness, scrupulosity, self-sacrifice, a world
> entirely different from this, which we leave in order to be
> born into this world, *before perhaps returning to the other to
> live once again beneath the sway of those unknown laws which
> we have obeyed because we bore their precepts in our hearts,
> knowing not whose hand had traced them there*—those laws to
> which every profound work of the intellect brings us nearer
> and nearer and which are invisible only—and still !—to fools.
> So that the idea that Bergotte was not wholly and permanently
> dead is by no means improbable.
>
> They buried him, but all through the night of mourning, in
> the lighted windows, his books arranged three by three, kept
> watch like angels with outspread wings and seemed, for him
> who was no more, the symbol of his resurrection.[1]

He hunts his quarry in that strange land between sleeping and
waking, in the pre-conscious gaps between the subconscious
and the fully conscious minds ; but without ever capturing it.

> Because the dream-world is not the waking world, it does
> not follow that the waking world is less genuine, far from
> it. . . . But are there perhaps other worlds more real than
> the waking world ? . . . By varying the room, the place
> at which we go to sleep . . . we succeed in producing a

[1] *The Captive*, pp. 250-1.

thousand times as many varieties of sleep as a gardener could
produce of carnations or roses. Gardeners produce flowers
that are delicious dreams, and others too that are like
nightmares. . . . Already this dream was beginning to fade
away. In attempting to recall it in order to portray it, I made
it fade all the faster. My eyelids were no longer so firmly
sealed over my eyes. If I tried to reconstruct my dream, they
opened completely. At every moment we must choose
between health and sanity on the one hand, and spiritual
pleasures on the other. I have always taken the cowardly part
of chosing the former.[1]

So in due course he turns to another field of mental activity,
which may perhaps prove more fruitful. In his passionate
attempt to analyse in order to control his memory, and even
more important his lack of memory—those strange lapses of
memory which haunt us all—he finds, like Freud, that memory
will not operate at the behest of the conscious will. He tries
to evoke the images of those he has loved, only to find that,
the love having died, the once beloved no longer live even
in memory. It is not the crucial point, for example, that his
grandmother, whom he had so adored, has died. What is
far more significant to him is that the intense love he bore
her as a child and a boy has gradually faded as his grief for
her has been eroded or ousted by other, newer, more violent
emotions. And this experience causes him to coin the curiously
lyrical term, " *les intermittences du cœur* " (the intermissions of
the heart) which always seems to me the verbal counterpart
of that exquisite small tune of Couperin's as enchantingly
entitled " *Les Barricades Mystérieuses.*" And Marcel scales his
mysterious barricade with dramatic, almost tragic sudden-
ness when he returns for the second time to Balbec, after his
grandmother's death, and once again occupies the bedroom
adjacent to hers on their first visit. To say that he then

[1] *The Captive*, pp. 159-63.

and parallel series—without loss of continuity, immediately
after the first evening at Balbec long ago, that I clung to the
minute in which my grandmother had leaned over me. The
self that I then was, that had so long disappeared, was once
again so close to me that I seemed still to hear the words
that had just been spoken, albeit they were nothing more
now than an illusion, as a man who is half awake thinks he
can still make out close at hand the sounds of his receding
dream. I was nothing now but the person who sought a
refuge in his grandmother's arms, sought to wipe away the
traces of his suffering by giving her kisses, that person whom
I should have had as great difficulty in imagining when I was
one or other of those persons which, for some time past, I
had successively been, as the efforts, doomed in any event to
sterility, that I should now have had to make to feel the
desires and joys of any of those which, for a time at least, I
no longer was. I reminded myself how, an hour before the
moment at which my grandmother had stooped down like
that, in her dressing gown, to unfasten my boots, as I
wandered along the stiflingly hot street, past the pastry-cook's,
I had felt that I could never, in my need to feel her arms
round me, live through the hour I had still to spend without
her. And now that this same need was reviving in me, I
knew that I might wait hour after hour, that she would
never again be by my side. I had only just discovered this
because I had only just, on feeling her for the first time,
alive, authentic, making my heart swell to breaking-point,
on finding her at last, learned that I had lost her forever.
Lost for ever ; I could not understand and was struggling to
bear the anguish of this contradiction : on the one hand an
existence, an affection, surviving in me as I had known them,
that is to say, created for me, a love in whose eyes everything
found in me so entirely its complement, its goal, its constant
lodestar, that the genius of great men, all the genius that
might have existed from the beginning of the world would
have been less precious to my grandmother than a single one
of my defects ; and on the other hand, as soon as I had lived

over again that bliss, as though it were present, feeling it
shot through by the certainty, throbbing like a physical
anguish, of an annihilation that had effaced my image of that
affection, had destroyed that existence, abolished in retrospect
our interwoven destiny, made of my grandmother at the
moment when I found her again as in a mirror, a mere
stranger whom chance had allowed to spend a few years in
my company, as it might have been in anyone else's, but to
whom, before and after those years, I was, I could be nothing.[1]

The evocation of his grandmother was neither a mere trick
of memory nor was it dependent on his will. It happened
as he bent down to unlace his boots, in a moment when he
was overcome by physical fatigue and was mentally off his
guard, just as he was off his guard when hovering between
sleeping and waking. When the moment came, he was able
deliberately to prolong it, by a species of auto-hypnosis, a
psychological discipline he had discovered and attempted to
develop in himself over a number of years. This particular
discipline which is common to all those gifted with paranormal
faculties, the so-called " sensitives," consists in dissociating the
subconsciousness from the shackles normally imposed on it
by the censorship of the conscious mind. And it was through
the practise of this discipline or technique that Proust was led
to the spiritual heights whence he was to look down on and
at last know himself integrally.

Perhaps the most famous passage in the whole of *A La
Recherche du Temps Perdu* occurs right at the beginning of
Du Côté de Chez Swann. If one may not too inappropriately
use the analogy of the technique of detective-story writing, it
is the first clue to the mystery (in this case, more accurately,
to the mystique) of the entire work. Here is it :

   . . . one day in winter, as I came home, my mother, seeing
   that I was cold, offered me some tea, a thing I did not ordinarily

[1] *Cities of the Plain*, vol. i, pp. 217–21.

take. I declined at first, and then, for no particular reason, changed my mind. She sent out for one of those short, plump little cakes called " petites madeleines " which look as though they had been moulded in the fluted scallop of a pilgrim's shell. And soon, mechanically, weary after a dull day with the prospect of a depressing to-morrow, *I raised to my lips a spoonful of the tea in which I had soaked a morsel of the cake. No sooner had the warm liquid, and the crumbs with it, touched my palate, than a shudder ran through my whole body, and I stopped, intent upon the extraordinary changes that were taking place. An exquisite pleasure had invaded my senses, but individual, detached, with no suggestion of its origin. And at once the vicissitudes of life had become indifferent to me, its disasters innocuous, its brevity illusory*—this new sensation having on me the effect which love has, of filling me with a precious essence ; or rather *the essence was not in me, it was myself.* I had ceased, now, to feel mediocre, accidental, mortal. Whence could it have come to me, this all-powerful joy ? I was conscious that it was connected with the taste of tea and cake, but that it infinitely transcended those savours, could not, indeed, be of the same nature as theirs. Whence did it come ? What did it signify ? How could I seize upon and define it ? . . . It is plain that the object of my quest, the truth, lies not in the cup but in myself. . . . I put down my cup and examine my own mind. . . . What an abyss of uncertainty, when the mind feels that some part of it has strayed beyond its own borders ; when it, *the seeker, is at once the dark region through which it must go seeking*, where all its equipment will avail it nothing. Seek ? More than that : create. It is face to face with *something which does not so far exist, to which it alone can give reality and substance, which it alone can bring into the light of day.*[1]

After describing several abortive attempts to discover what is happening in his mind, he continues :

I compel my mind to make one further effort, to follow and recapture once again the fleeting sensation. And that

[1] *Swann's Way*, vol. i, pp. 58 *et seq.*

nothing may interrupt it in its course, I shut out every obstacle, every extraneous idea, I stop my ears and inhibit all attention to the sounds which come from the next room. And then, feeling that my mind is growing fatigued without having any success to report, I compel it to think of other things, to rest and refresh itself before the supreme attempt. And then for the second time I clear an empty space in front of it. I place in position before my mind's eye the still recent taste of the first mouthful, and *I feel something start within me, something that leaves its resting-place and attempts to rise, something that has been embedded like an anchor at a great depth* ; I do not yet know what it is, but I can feel it mounting slowly ; I can measure the resistance, I can hear the echo of great spaces traversed. . . .

Ten times he tries to raise

" the image, the visual memory which being linked to that taste, has tried to follow it into my conscious mind. . . ." And suddenly the memory returns. The taste was of the little crumb of madeleine which on Sunday mornings at Combray . . . my aunt Leonie used to give me, dipping it first in her own cup . . . but when from a long-distant past nothing subsists, after the people are dead, after the things are broken and scattered, still, alone, more fragile, but with more vitality, more unsubstantial, more persistent, more faithful, the smell and taste of things remain poised a long time, like souls, ready to remind us, waiting and hoping for their moment, amid the ruins of all the rest ; and bear unfalteringly, in the tiny and almost impalpable drop of their essence, the vast structure of recollection. . . .

And just as the Japanese amuse themselves by filling a porcelain bowl with water, and steeping in it little crumbs of paper which until then are without character and form, but, the moment they become wet, stretch themselves and bend, take on colour and distinctive shape . . . so in that moment all the flowers in our garden and in M. Swann's park, and the water-lilies on the Vivonne and the good folk of the village and their little dwellings and the parish church and the whole of Combray and of its surroundings, taking their proper shapes and growing solid, sprang into being, town and gardens alike, from my cup of tea.

At this stage he does not pursue the analysis of this experience further. It has enabled him to rebuild the Combray scene, and this, he now proceeds to do, recreating at the same time himself as a child, his family and their friends, and so gradually leading into the plot of the " outward " story, with the theme of Swann's love affair. From this initial impetus the novel flows on as a novel. But in the last volume, *Le Temps Retrouvé*, the leitmotif of the madeleine and the cup of tea will be taken up again and fully developed. The construction, as we shall then see, bears a resemblance to that of the detective story, in so far as the author only reveals his clues to the reader gradually, piecemeal, scattered amongst the more ordinary sections of his narrative. But, like the master of the detective novel, he is actually working backwards, not forwards. His plan is based on the final chapter, the revelation of what " actually happened " ; but he is not ready to disclose this nor to discuss it until he has unfolded his plot, developed his characters, and particularly himself. Not until the " Je " has chased the " Moi " through all those hundreds of pages, as in the detective story the detective has chased the murderer and finally caught up with him, is it possible for Proust to divulge the secrets of the " Moi," as the thriller-writer on the last page or two reveals the motive for the murder.

When he tasted the little madeleine dipped in tea, his emotional response was, he tells us, one of exquisite pleasure, swiftly followed by the intellectual realisation that the " precious essence " with which it seemed to fill him was not in himself, but *was himself*. He accepts the experience— the contact so suddenly and unexpectedly established between

[1] *Swann's Way*, vol. i, p. 62.

his conscious memory and his subconscious retention—as an invitation, more, as an urgent compulsion, to seek and to create.

In order to seek, he used a technique which resembles that of the trance-medium or the clairvoyant. He attempts to isolate his conscious mind from all outside contacts and impressions, to coax it into becoming relaxed, passive; and in this, after intensive and patient efforts, he succeeds. The first experiment does not take him very far into the past, into his subconsciousness "whence something attempts to rise, something that has been embedded like an anchor, at a great depth." It does succeed partially, even brilliantly as far as it goes, for it gives him Combray, it starts him on his creative task. This is undoubtedly an important and successful result, but it is by no means all; there is more, much more, to be discovered still.

But from this moment onwards, Proust will never again lose contact with his subconscious. He has found a clue to happiness, though as yet he does not know in what, precisely, that happiness consists; nor what message the experience and the delightful emotions it evokes is trying to convey to him. He is not yet ready to receive it. He knows, however, that he cannot actively provoke the initial stimulus, that he must receive it, passively, when it comes to him, through his sense-perceptions, in its own good time, over which his will and his conscious mind have no control. But now he is always on the alert for a repetition of the experience.

He describes an earlier occurrence of it towards the end of the first volume of *Du Côté de Chez Swann*. He is still writing here of his childhood. At this time his asthmatic ailment had not yet revealed itself. On his visits to Combray he revelled in the sights and sounds of the countryside; in the quality of the sunlight on an old wall, the movement of the water on the Vivonne, in trees, flowers, and ancient churches. He

felt then an obscure, budding desire to put these impressions
into words, on paper ; but they seemed to him not sufficiently
solid nor deep to justify his desire, even at that tender age,
to become a writer.   However, one day, when on a drive
with the old family friend, Dr. Percepied, he has another
exciting experience. He sees the spires of the churches of
Martinville and of Vieuxvicq, performing a curious series of
movements, apparently, as the carriage rushes along the
country road :

> they reminded me of three young girls in an old legend,
> abandoned in a solitary landscape already darkened by the
> falling twilight ; and as we galloped onwards, I watched
> them timidly seeking their way, and, after a few clumsy
> stumbles of their noble outlines, huddle together, then glide
> one behind the other, appearing on the sky, which was still
> pink, only as one dark, charming, and resigned silhouette,
> finally to disappear in the night.

In describing this experience the adult author has quoted
his first childish attempt at writing. For, he says,

> without saying to myself that what was hidden behind the
> spires of Martinville must be something like a pretty turn of
> phrase, for it was in the form of words that gave me pleasure
> that it had appeared to me, asking the doctor for a pencil and
> a piece of paper, in spite of the jolting of the carriage, in order
> to lighten my conscience and obedient to the enthusiasm that
> urged me on, I composed the following little piece which I
> have since found again, and which I have only had to alter
> slightly.

Then follows the little essay from which I have quoted in the
preceding paragraph.

So right at the beginning we are told that when he consciously set out to compose, to write, he found himself
inhibited by some psychological cause the reason of which he
could not fathom.   This inability to express himself lay heavily

on his conscience. All the more was he filled with happiness and exhilaration on the very rare occasions when suddenly an impression, reaching down to and awakening something in his subconscious, released his creative faculty. He is always on the alert for a repetition of this strange experience. The next description of it, however, contains an element of frustration, as well as a repetition of the triad pattern.

It occurs at the beginning of *A l'Ombre des Jeunes Filles en Fleurs*. He is on his first visit to Balbec with his grandmother, where they meet her old school-friend, Mme de Villeparisis, who takes Marcel on a drive through the surrounding countryside. And on this drive he sees three trees, which appear to be beckoning to him, mysteriously.

> We came down towards Hudimesnil; suddenly I was overwhelmed with that profound happiness which I had not often felt since Combray; happiness analogous to that which had been given me by—among other things—the steeples of Martinville. But this time it remained incomplete. I had just seen, standing a little way back from the steep ridge over which we were passing, three trees, probably marking the entrance to a shady avenue, which made a pattern at which I was looking now not for the first time; I could not succeed in reconstructing the place from which they had been, as it were, detached, but I felt that it had been familiar to me once; *so that my mind having wavered between some distant year and the present moment*, Balbec and its surroundings began to dissolve and I asked myself whether the whole of this drive were not a make-believe, Balbec a place to which I had never gone save in imagination, Mme de Villeparisis a character in a story and the three old trees the reality which one recaptures on raising one's eyes from the book which one has been reading and which describes an environment into which one has come to believe that one has been bodily transported.[1]

I have italicised the important clue in this passage—" my

[1] *Within a Budding Grove*, vol. ii, p. 20.

mind wavered," [1] to which we shall return in due course. He
continues :

> I looked at the three trees ; I could see them plainly, but
> my mind felt that they were concealing something which it
> had not grasped, as when things are placed out of our reach,
> so that our fingers, stretched out at arm's-length, can only
> touch for a moment their outer surface, and can take hold of
> nothing. Then we rest for a little while before thrusting out
> our arm with refreshed vigour, and trying to reach an inch
> or two farther. But if my mind was thus to collect itself, to
> gather strength, I should have to be alone. What would I
> not have given to be able to escape as I used to do on those
> walks along the Guermantes way, when I detached myself
> from my parents ! It seemed indeed that I ought to do so
> now. I recognised that kind of pleasure which requires, it
> is true, a certain effort on the part of the mind, but in com-
> parison with which the attractions of the inertia which inclines
> us to renounce that pleasure seem very slight. That pleasure
> the object of which I could but dimly feel, that pleasure which
> I must create for myself, I experienced only on rare occasions,
> but on each of these it seemed to me that the things which
> had happened in the interval were of but scant importance,
> and that in attaching myself to the reality of that pleasure
> alone I could at length begin to lead a new life. I laid my
> hand for a moment across my eyes, so as to be able to shut
> them without Mme de Villeparisis's noticing. I sat there,
> thinking of nothing, then with my thoughts collected, com-
> pressed and strengthened I sprang farther forward in the
> direction of the trees, or rather in that inverse direction at
> the end of which I could see them growing within myself.
> I felt again behind them the same object, known to me and
> yet vague, which I could not bring nearer. And yet all three
> of them, as the carriage moved on, I could see coming towards
> me. Where had I looked at them before ? [2]

---

[1] I would prefer " stumbled " to " wavered." The French text is as follows :
" *de sorte que mon esprit ayant trébuché entre quelque aunée lointaine et le moment présent.*"
[2] *Within a Budding Grove,* vol. ii, pp. 20 *et seq.*

By the time the reader has reached the last volume of *Le Temps Retrouvé* so much else has happened that he can be forgiven if he has by then forgotten all about the " *petite madeleine* " and its vast symbolic significance, and if he, too, has missed the prophetic intimations which the three trees were trying to impart to him, as well as to the author. But perhaps, like a master of detective fiction, Proust has deliberately distracted our minds from the main theme, as in the thriller the author, by judicious planting of " red herrings," tries to distract the reader from guessing " whodunit " until the very last page. However that may be, whether Proust did it deliberately or not, when his main theme is at last taken up again, at the door of the mansion of the Princesse de Guermantes, so very many years later, it has all the novelty, the shock-impact on the reader, of the last paragraph of a detective story, or of a *coup-de-théâtre*, a superb curtain, on the spectators at the play. And just as the ultimate discovery in the thriller allows the author to give the reader his explanation of the whole mysterious business, so, now that his story has been told, Proust at last enlarges on his leitmotif at length. The moment of release has come ; his resistances and repressions have been resolved in the classical Freudian manner by a " stumble " which, this time, makes the contact between his subconscious retentiveness and his conscious mind, firmly and permanently ; by which the " Je " and the " Moi " are finally united, integrated, and are enabled to attain that peace and harmony he had been seeking during so many weary years of physical and mental agony, of apparent frustration, but which are now suddenly proved not to have been lost or wasted, but to have been—whilst he who had lived and suffered through them had remained in ignorance of their purpose—subconsciously rich and fruitful beyond all expectation.

The " outward " story is finished. Marcel has returned to Paris from a nursing home, where he had vainly been seeking a cure for his physical ailments. He has been away a long time. He is wretchedly miserable, ailing, and without further hope of recovery now. He is weighed down by ill-health, and a sense of utter failure as a writer. He has not yet started on that novel which was to have vindicated all his past " laziness " and atoned for his constant surrender to the attractions of the line of least resistance. For these reasons, paradoxically, he decides to accept an invitation to a musical afternoon party given by the Princesse de Guermantes (who, incidentally, turns out to be, finally and triumphantly, our old friend and enemy, the *çi-devant* Mme Verdurin !)

I told myself it was really not worth while to deprive myself of society, since I was either not equipped for or not up to the precious " work " to which I had for so long been hoping to devote myself " to-morrow " and which, maybe, corresponded to no reality. . . .

Reviewing the painful reflections of which I have just been speaking, I had entered the courtyard of the Guermantes' mansion and in my distraction, I had not noticed an approaching carriage ; at the call of the link-man I had barely time to draw quickly to one side, and in stepping backwards *I stumbled* against some unevenly placed paving-stones behind which there was a coach-house. As I recovered myself, one of my feet stepped on a flagstone lower than the one next to it. In that instant, all my discouragement disappeared, and I was possessed by the same felicity which at different moments of my life had been given me by the view of trees which had seemed familiar to me during the drive round Balbec, the view of the belfries of Martinville, the savour of a madeleine dipped in a cup of tea. . . . As at the moment when I tasted the madeleine, all my apprehensions about the future, all my intellectual doubts, were dissipated. Those doubts, which had assailed me just before, regarding the reality of my literary gifts, and even regarding the reality of literature itself, were dispersed as though by magic. This time, I vowed that I should not resign myself to ignoring why, without any fresh reasoning, without any definite hypothesis, the insoluble difficulties of the previous instant had lost all importance ; as was the case when I had tasted a madeleine dipped in a cup of tea. The felicity which I now experienced was undoubtedly the same as that which I had felt when I ate the madeleine, the cause of which I had then postponed seeking. There was only a material difference in the images evoked. A deep azure intoxicated my eyes, a feeling of freshness, of dazzling light, enveloped me, and in my desire to seize upon and hold down these impressions, just as I had not dared to move when I ate the madeleine, because of trying to conjure back that of which it reminded me, I stood, doubtless an object of ridicule to the link-men, repeating the movement of a moment ago, one foot upon the higher flagstone, the other on the lower one. Merely repeating the movement was useless ; but, if, oblivious of the Guermantes' reception, I succeeded in recapturing the sensation which accompanied the movement, again the intoxicating and elusive vision softly pervaded me, as though it said : " Grasp me as I float by you, if you can, and try to solve the enigma of the happiness I offer you." And then, all at once, I recognised that Venice which my descriptive efforts and pretended snapshots of memory had failed to recall ; the sensation I had once felt on two uneven slabs in the Baptistery of Saint Mark had been given back to me, and was linked with all the other sensations of that and other days which had lingered expectantly in their places among the series of forgotten years from which a sudden chance had imperiously called them forth. So, too, the taste of the little madeleine had recalled Combray. But how was it that these visions of Combray and of Venice at one and another moment had caused me a joyous certainty, sufficient, without other proofs, to make the thought of death indifferent to me ? Asking myself this, and resolved to find the answer that very day, I entered the Guermantes' mansion. . . . [1]

Here he finds a concert in progress. On the Princess's instructions (Madame Verdurin still takes her music seriously !)

[1] *Time Regained*, pp. 210–11.

re-establish the buried link between the conscious "Je" and the subconscious "Moi." This experience alone could give him complete happiness, based on the breaking-down of his anxiety neurosis and its replacement by a sense of security. And this spiritual security, independent of and free from the infirmities of the body and the mind, could only be found "outside Time," in the extra-temporal sphere. For the essence of the experience was, as he describes it himself, a spiritual one, and although he continued to disclaim all belief or faith in the narrower sense, and practised no religious discipline, the ecstasy that filled him on these rare occasions was comparable to the religious ecstasy of the great mystics.

As the result of this transcendental experience he has at last made conscious contact with Eternity, and having found Eternity he is now able to integrate the "Je" and the "Moi" that jointly contain his past selves, his present, and also his future. He has found the key to recapture, not only Past Time, all his own past times, but beyond Lost Time he has rediscovered his Lost Self, the fourth-dimensional quintessence of the Self, emancipated from Time's thrall.

> If I thought that Bergotte had spoken falsely when he referred to the joys of spiritual life, it was because I then gave the name of spiritual life to logical reasonings which had no relation with it, which had no relation with what now existed in me—just as I found society and life wearisome because I was judging them from memories without Truth ; whilst now that a true moment of the past had been born again in me three separate times, *I had such a desire to live.*

For that is the immediate practical result of the great spiritual experience, when once he has brought his conscious mind and will to examine it and analyse it out. For now he has found the will-power, the courage, the zest for living which until then he had so lamentably lacked ; the lack of which was due to the repressed sense of guilt and shame

outwardly expressed as " laziness " and " lack of will-power "
of his consciousness divorced from the directing power of the
subconscious ; the " Je " lost in Time, because of the barrier
between it and the " Moi " which was its sole means of
contact with Eternity.

All his doubts, hesitations, anxieties and frustrations have
now disappeared, as the result of his one great moment of
self-revelation, with its affectual sense of happiness amounting
to ecstasy, strong enough to enable him to overcome all the
misery of the past. Now he has the determination and the
mental energy to create ; the belief in his powers, as well as
in his talent. The fear of death of the " Je " which was
unreal, because it masked the reluctance of the " Je " to face
the realities of life without the inner, spiritual support of the
" Moi," has now been replaced by a new and ardent desire
to live. He thinks he is happy because he has conquered Time,
which he has for so long equated with Death ; but it is probably
equally true that his happiness was due to the fact that he had at
last found himself, had become a whole person, for the first
time a complete living entity, capable of action and creation.

From the moment when he describes this experience, the
later pages of Le Temps Retrouvé are written with a new
firmness and vitality, although he did not live long enough
to make the final corrections to them. For, unfortunately,
his physical health really was declining rapidly, he was gravely
ill ; and although he found the key that opened for him the
flood-gates of creation, not too late, but just in time, the next
sixteen years of his life, dedicated to his great work, were an
endless battle to hold off Death, conquered in the spirit, but
still a permanent menace to the feeble body, the exhausted
constitution.

In the final pages of Le Temps Retrouvé Proust describes his
plan of work and the difficulties which he clearly foresaw
facing the execution of it. These pages seem to me to rank

every moment, still, I had to drag it along with me, that it
sustained me, that I was perched up on it, on its dizzying
height, and that I could not move without moving it with me.

The date on which I had heard the tinkling of the bell on
the garden-gate at Combray, so distant and yet so close within
me, was a point of rest in that enormous dimension which I
did not know I contained. I was dizzy from looking down
below me and into myself, to see all those years within me,
as if they had been miles below me.

I understood now, why the Duc de Guermantes, whom,
when I had seen him sitting in a chair, I had admired for
having aged so little, although he had so many more years
below him than I had, as soon as he had risen and tried to
stand up, had wobbled on his legs, reedy as those of old
archbishops, surrounded by a crowd of young seminarists,
about whom there is no longer anything solid except their
cross of metal, and had only been able to come forward,
trembling like a leaf on top of his not easily borne height of
eighty-three years, as if men were perched on living stilts,
which never stop growing, sometimes higher than steeples,
which finally make walking difficult and dangerous for them,
and from which, suddenly, they tumble down. I was afraid
to think that mine were already so high under my feet, and
it did not seem to me that I would still have the strength to
keep attached to myself that past that already went so deep
down, and that I carried so painfully within me! If at least
enough time was left to me to finish my work, I would not
fail to stamp it with the seal of that Time, the idea of which
imposed itself on me with such force to-day, and in it I
would describe men, even if it were to make them seem like
monstrous creatures, as occupying in Time a considerably
bigger place than that, so limited, which is reserved to them
in space; on the contrary, a place immeasurably prolonged,
since, simultaneously, they reach out, like giants rooted in the
years, to the past times they have lived through, so far
away—between which so many days have come to take their
places—in Time.

INDEX